# Exhibitions
## AND
# Trade Shows

### The step-by-step guide to
### MAKING A PROFIT from exhibiting

## S. IVAN JURISEVIC

Prentice
Hall

Pearson Education Australia
Unit 4, Level 2
14 Aquatic Drive
Frenchs Forest NSW 2086

www.pearsoned.com.au

Commissioning Editor: Mark Stafford
Senior Project Editor: Carolyn Robson
Copy Editor: Catherine Hammond
Cover and internal design by Liz Seymour
Cover photograph: Getty Images
Typeset by Midland Typesetters, Maryborough, Vic.

Printed in Australia by Griffin Press

1 2 3 4 5 06 05 04 03 02

National Library of Australia
Cataloguing-in-Publication Data

Jurisevic, Ivan.
Exhibitions and trade shows: the step-by-step guide to
making a profit from exhibiting.

    Includes index.
    ISBN 1 74009 763 7.

    1. Exhibitions – Handbooks, manuals, etc. 2. Trade shows –
    Handbooks, manuals, etc. I. Title.

659.152

An imprint of Pearson Education Australia

# Contents

# Acknowledgements

So much more time and effort goes into writing a book than I imagined when I set out to write this, my first one. And in that long process I came to an important realisation: it is not just 'my' book; many people have contributed to it, over a very long period of time, and some of them need special mention.

First of all, I would like to thank my clients. It is you who were the impetus, back in 1990, to expand my services beyond stand design and construction, and it is from the experience of working with you over the years that the information in this book has grown. In a very real sense it is *your* book.

In particular I would like to thank Daryl and Julie Sursok at Extended Sampling, who started as clients over ten years ago and have become friends, for the way that they understood and made allowances for the time that I was devoting to the writing of this book, during a period when we were also working together on their new projects.

Thanks to Hugh McCreath, now retired, who gave me my first job in the exhibition industry when he invited me to join his company, ADS, in 1986, and from whom I learnt about the industry over the following three years, and for long after I set up on my own. And many thanks to Grant Gosson and Brian Farrar at Display by Design, who have provided outstanding service, both to myself and to my clients, over the years.

The crew at Pearson Education, Mark Stafford, Carolyn Robson and Lemonia Kormas, have been a delightful revelation. Having heard horror stories about the dealings that other writers have had with their publishers I went in braced for battle, but they have been unfailingly professional in their commitment to getting the best for the book, generous and understanding when I missed deadlines due to work commitments and a true pleasure to work with.

Wendy Evans deserves special thanks, because she has been a never-ending source of encouragement, and has drawn generously on her experience of writing her own books, including *How to Get New Business in 90 Days and Keep it Forever*, in putting me, and keeping me, on track.

There is a level of gratitude that cannot be expressed in words to my family, who have loved, supported and encouraged me, not only in this project, but in so many ways over the years; in particular Paula Masselos, my son Anton, my brother Marlan Jurisevic and (yes, I'm going to thank my mum!) Emma Jurisevic.

There are many more individuals – family, friends and business associates in and out of the exhibition industry – whom I would like to thank personally, but if I started I would have to keep going for another chapter. I hope you understand. You know who you are. Thank you.

# Introduction

## How to have a good show—make a profit!

Exhibiting is a branch of marketing. In fact, modern exhibitions and trade shows are descended from the ancient markets that have been a part of the business of being human since antiquity.

But modern exhibiting is expensive. There is no cheap way of taking part in an exhibition these days. The question is: *How can you justify the expense?* The answer is: *With a profit*.

And exhibitions can be very profitable, indeed. Many companies find that exhibitions are the most cost-effective part of their whole marketing mix. That is, they get the greatest return on their marketing dollar from shows. They find that the couple of months after a show are the busiest— and the most rewarding!—of the year's sales activity.

The reason is simple. If you are in a good show, there are more buyers concentrated there than anywhere else. In the final analysis, that is what a good exhibition delivers: a high concentration of buyers. The rest you have to deliver yourself.

This book is about how to deliver.

## How did this book come about?

The system of exhibiting described here was first developed in 1990 as a response to the needs of my clients. I had been building exhibition stands for them since 1986, but it had become clear that, rather than more award-winning stands, what many of my clients and their staff urgently needed was better skills in dealing with show visitors.

As a result, I drew on my years of experience as a trainer and put together a pilot workshop. This was developed with my clients and experienced exhibition industry professionals. With their feedback and help we worked on it until we had an effective system.

Over the years since then, that system has been continually improved in the best way possible—through practical application. It was used in shows and what worked was kept; what didn't was discarded.

The end result is the book that you hold in your hands. It is the summation of the best experience of hundreds of companies. *It works*. When companies apply it, almost without exception they achieve outstanding improvements in results. I trust that you will, too.

# How to use this book

This book is a step-by-step instruction manual on how to exhibit.

It covers a 12-month period of activity, from the initial choosing and planning of a show, right through all the steps of exhibiting, to the final return-on-investment analysis, at which point you can make a rational decision as to whether to attend the show again, based on some hard figures.

The easiest way to use this book is to first read Chapter 1, *Strategy and tactics*. This gives you a broad understanding of what you will be doing. It outlines the whole system, summarising strategy and tactics, and giving you an overview of the 12-month, step-by-step process.

The rest of the book, Chapters 2 through 14, covers those steps in detail. You may want to dip into this material at the outset, if there are some areas you find particularly interesting.

But the main task here is to write the dates for the various steps into your diary, working forwards and backwards from an exhibition to which you want to apply the system.

Then put the book away.

Later, when you come to the diary entries related to the steps, go back to the book, read the relevant sections in detail and implement what they suggest.

# The 80/20 rule in exhibiting

Bear in mind that the various times recommended for some of the activities are only indicative. Your timetable may vary. For example, the exhibitor manuals supplied by organisers come at different times and decisions as to what to display may be determined by when equipment will become available, and so on.

Naturally, if you have a show coming up in less than 12 months, you may have to leave out some activities and compress others into a shorter time span.

The following activities, however, are crucial to a successful exhibition, and they cannot be left out without severely impairing the results you can expect to get.

1. Before the show, draw up your personal invitation lists and invite the people on them to your stand.
2. Before the show, train your staff in product knowledge and in the skills of managing show visitors.
3. During the show, gather leads by systematically interviewing visitors and recording the details on lead forms.
4. After the show, follow up those leads systematically, in order of importance.

Each of these activities is described in detail in this book. They are the expression of the 80/20 rule in exhibiting, and they constitute the 20% of activity that will get you 80% of the results. If your company is like most companies I have worked with, the result will be a dramatic improvement in your sales figures.

## Who is this book addressing?

This book is addressed to the person who is in charge of managing an exhibition. In my experience, that is either the owner of a company or a manager who has been assigned the job. And since you are reading the book, I presume that is you. So I will be addressing you throughout the book as the one in charge of the whole show, from beginning to end.

This is not to say that the work will not be shared. A show is a team effort requiring close cooperation. But, in my experience, unless there is one person who is ultimately responsible to ensure that each step happens, jobs fall between stools, and the exhibition does not achieve its potential.

If you are in charge, then I suggest you share the contents of this book with your team. People work better when they understand the game plan and where they and their colleagues fit in to make it happen.

## More free information!

As part of the ongoing service that you get as a result of your purchase of this book, you are welcome to subscribe to the *Showright Bulletin*. This will be sent to you as a regular email, and each issue covers a subject that may be useful to the success of your exhibiting activity and keep you up-to-date with useful new approaches you might like to try.

It is free, and you can log on and confirm your subscription on www.showright.com.

# Dedication

For Anton

Thank you, my darling boy, for all those times over the long months that I was writing this book when you wanted to spend time with me but patiently put up with your dad being glued to the computer and shooing you off.

And for occasionally jumping on me (well, often, actually) and reminding me why I was doing it!

So here it is! Mission accomplished! Let's party!

# Chapter 1

# Strategy and tactics

- Strategy—to use the exhibition as a filtering process to gain new clients

- The four levels of filtering

- The end result of the filtering process

- Tactics—making it happen

# Strategy—to use the exhibition as a filtering process to gain new clients

The purpose of exhibiting is to gain new clients. That is the approach taken in this book.

For most companies an exhibition is a marketing activity that has to be justified by an adequate return on the marketing dollar that has been invested in it. The main way this will happen is through sales to new clients. Sales to existing clients will generally not provide an adequate return since, unless one is up-selling or cross-selling, sales to existing clients would likely have been made in any case.

This is not to say that there are no good reasons for exhibiting other than to gain new clients, but none of them are incompatible with making new sales. Chapter 2, *Twelve months before the show*, examines this point in detail.

The main reason that exhibitions are valuable as a marketing medium is the high concentration of potential clients. However, not everyone at an exhibition is a potential client for every company that is exhibiting. For instance, at a mining show a company that manufactures respirators will be interested in talking to safety officers. But safety officers make up only a small proportion of the visitors attending the show. Furthermore, they are not readily identifiable as safety officers until one gets to talk to them.

So how does a company most effectively get to those people who make up its target market?

Strategically, one of the most useful approaches is to think of an exhibition as a progressive filtering process.

# The four levels of filtering

The filtering process can be split into four areas:

1. The organiser
2. The stand
3. The stand staff
4. The post-show follow-up.

## The first level of filtering is the organiser

An exhibition happens within a certain catchment area. This may be local, regional, national or international, depending on the show. Within that catchment area, the exhibition is focused to appeal to a specific target group. In trade shows the focus is generally on a particular area of industry or on a professional area. For instance, a mining show targets people involved in the mining industry, a fire safety show focuses on fire officers across industries and an accounting show focuses on accountants.

A public show, on the other hand, is a consumer show aimed at the general public. Examples are gardening, home improvement and home computer shows.

The organiser of the show promotes it within the catchment area, using a variety of means that include direct mail, advertising in industry journals, in the popular press, on television and so on. By these means the organiser persuades people who have an interest in the field to come through the doors.

In other words, the organiser filters out of the general population those people who are interested in the show's focus and, hopefully, in individual exhibitors. As a result, there is a higher concentration of potential clients walking around in the aisles than on the streets. That is the central attraction of exhibitions.

However, as was mentioned above, not everyone in the aisles is a potential client for every exhibitor. So, for a show that has 10,000 visitors, 1,000 could potentially become a particular exhibitor's clients. Or it could be 500 or 5,000.

But, as they walk past the stand, they all look the same. How to attract them?

## The second level of filtering is the exhibition stand

The primary purpose of an exhibition stand is to filter *onto* it those people who are prospective clients, and to filter *off* it those who are not.

The main way of doing this is, obviously, to have on display the product or service that the company is selling, in the hope that prospective customers will stop and give the company's representatives a chance to speak with them.

There are a variety of ways that a company can increase the attractiveness of its display to stop its target market. These are discussed later in the book. One activity, however, is outstanding in its effectiveness in attracting potential new clients: demonstrations of products and services.

As one walks around a show and notes where people are gathered, it is almost invariably where there is an activity of some sort going on. This can take many forms. It may be entertainment such as a juggler provides, or some interaction between visitors and staff, or a demonstration of the company's product or service.

While they can all attract a large number of people, the first two are non-specific: they draw everyone. But the demonstration of a product or service attracts a larger proportion of those who have an interest in it. Those who are not interested keep walking, which is desirable, because they are not the company's clients.

In other words, a demonstration of a company's product further filters a higher concentration of its potential clients to its stand.

How to demonstrate a product to best effect and how stand staff can best take advantage of this concentration of people are topics addressed in detail later in the book.

## The third level of filtering is the people who are staffing the stand

While there will be a higher concentration of potential clients amongst stand visitors, still not all of them are actually potential clients, and the role of stand staff is to further filter out of that concentration those who have a genuine interest in your product. They do this by interviewing them.

### To qualify or be qualified?

Most people who staff a stand take the approach that they are there in order to talk about their product to visitors. Yet it is far more effective, strategically, if they take the more proactive approach that they are there to interview the visitors to find out if they qualify as a potential client.

The conversation can then move in one of three directions. If the visitors don't qualify as buyers, they are bid a pleasant goodbye, and they move back into the passing stream. If they do qualify, the staff try to make a sale. If they are successful the company has a new client, which is great.

However, most companies make few or no sales on the stand; the bulk of them come after the show. It is for this reason that getting leads at an exhibition is the primary purpose for most companies. So the staff members' most important job is to record the visitors' details so that they can be followed up after the show, when the company representatives can again try to make a sale.

The above is not meant to suggest that staff should not always talk about their products and services and show them off to their best advantage. Of course they must do that. But time at a show is limited, and they will do better if they first ensure that they are talking to the right person.

In a good show there are going to be far more potential clients than staff can possibly get to. If they take a customer-focused approach rather than a product-focused approach, they can multiply many times the number of qualified leads they get. Of course, to be most effective, staff need to be trained, before the show, in how to interview visitors and in how to record the details of the conversation systematically and rank the visitors in order of importance, as some will be hotter prospects than others.

The subject of staff training is covered in detail in Chapter 7.

So now the company has a number of qualified leads, which is a further concentration of the show visitors. While not all of them will be buyers, a very high proportion will be. Those leads contain gold, yet most companies stop prospecting right there. They do not follow up.

## The fourth level of filtering is the post-show follow-up

As already noted, most companies make the bulk, if not all, of their sales after a show. Yet few companies have a systematic process of following up the leads they get at an exhibition. They are missing out on a lot of business.

There are a variety of ways to follow up leads after a show. To some extent, it depends on how they were collected. The various ways and their relative effectiveness are covered in detail later in the book, but let us note for now that the most effective, for most companies, is for the salespeople to follow the leads up personally in order of importance, as determined from the details the stand staff recorded on the lead forms at the time of the conversation. The importance of a lead form in providing a detailed, written record of what was said at the meeting on the stand cannot be over-emphasised.

The follow-up process is covered in Chapters 11 to 13.

# The end result of the filtering process

The end result of this process of steady concentration and filtering is an increased number of new clients and customers. Are all the leads going to result in sales? Of course not, but there will be a much higher proportion than if their collection and follow-up is done randomly or not at all.

How much of a difference can it make? As examples, clients have reported a 600% increase in qualified leads (these really are qualified leads, not put-your-card-in-the-fish-bowl-and-win-a-trip-to-Hawaii type leads), a tripling of sales, and a 30% increase in their market share.

## Tactics—making it happen

Tactics are the practical steps for bringing a strategy about. What follows here is an outline of those steps. The chapters at the end of each heading are those in which the steps are discussed in detail.

As earlier said, the idea is to work through the outline now in conjunction with your diary. Starting from your show date, work backwards and forwards, noting the dates of these steps in your diary. Later, when you come to each diary entry, go back to the book and read the appropriate section (in Chapters 2 to 14) and apply it.

Naturally, if you have a show coming up comparatively soon, you may have to compress some of these activities. It might even be too late to do some, or you may have done some already. Do what you can, and do more next time around. Each of these steps will improve your performance at a show; each will build on the last.

These are the crucial activities. Do them and you will get most of the results that you are going to get from the show. As was mentioned in the Introduction, this represents the 20% of activity that will get you 80% of the results.

1. Before the show, ring those people you specifically want to turn into clients and make an appointment to meet them on your stand.
2. Before the show, conduct a training session with your staff in which you refresh their knowledge of your products and services, and in which you also do a comparison between your services and your competitors'.
3. Before the show, train your stand staff, focusing on who, specifically, are the people you are after, and the specialised skills of interviewing and managing show visitors.
4. During the show, interview exhibition visitors in order to identify potential clients. Then either sell them your product on the spot or record their details so that you can follow them up after the show.
5. After the show, follow those people up systematically, in order of priority.

# The tactics, step by step

**TWELVE MONTHS BEFORE THE SHOW (Chapter 2)**

Plan the show

Decide on your reasons for exhibiting

Define your target market

Choose and assess a show

Choose a stand position

Will you make money? Analyse your resources

**SIX MONTHS BEFORE THE SHOW (Chapter 3)**

Meet with the exhibition management team to plan the show

Review the previous show

Set a target for the coming show

Prepare a budget

Decide on what you will display

Decide on your stand approach

Decide on promotional activity

Decide on dress for the show

Go through the exhibitor manual

Prepare a written action plan

**THREE MONTHS BEFORE THE SHOW (Chapter 4)**

Meet with the full show team

Prepare a preliminary roster

Prepare lists of potential clients for pre-show invitation

Confirm accommodation and travel arrangements

Plan pre-show training for staff

Design and print lead forms

**SIX WEEKS BEFORE THE SHOW (Chapter 5)**

Begin the pre-show invitation campaigns

Write the follow-up letters

**ONE MONTH BEFORE THE SHOW (Chapter 6)**

Finalise the stand roster and circulate it

Confirm all arrangements

Hire temporary staff

**TWO WEEKS BEFORE THE SHOW (Chapter 7)**
Reconfirm move-in details
Check that all resources and supplies are in hand
Check on your stand
Provide your staff with:
    Product training
    Product demonstrations
    Visitor management skills

**THE SHOW BUILD-UP (Chapter 8)**
Start your build-up at the first available moment
Meet the organiser
Personally monitor the progress of construction
Check on your competitors

**DURING THE SHOW (Chapter 9)**
Manage visitors
Coach staff
Maintain an up-to-date schedule
Keep an eye on the competition
Manage the stand
Learn from the show

**THE PULL-OUT (Chapter 10)**
Supervise the pull-out

**THE DAY AFTER THE SHOW (Chapter 11)**
Organising the post-show follow-up
Set up a database
Analyse the show

**FOR THE TWO WEEKS FOLLOWING THE SHOW (Chapter 12)**
Contact the leads from the show

**FOR TWO MONTHS AFTER THE SHOW (Chapter 13)**
Sell

**THREE MONTHS AFTER THE SHOW (Chapter 14)**
Do a return-on-investment analysis of the show
Review your targets and set new ones
Circulate a report on the results
Celebrate and reward success!

Chapter 2

# Twelve months before the show

# Planning the show

An exhibition is a cycle of activity that happens over a 12-month period.

Those few days at the show on which so much focus is put is only the pivot point around which a range of activity turns, if you want to achieve the potential of which a show is capable.

Planning your activity ahead of time will give you much better results and make your job easier. The show process will run more smoothly, you will have fewer problems, and you will achieve it all in a comparatively relaxed fashion.

These next two chapters are about planning a show. They outline a sequence of actions that others have used successfully, while offering reasons and advice along the way. Think of it as a kind of road atlas for an exhibition trip. Your job as the exhibition manager is to ensure that all the stops along the way are reached in a timely fashion.

This chapter deals with basic questions about choosing a show and why you want to go into it.

# Reasons for exhibiting

So why do we want to go into this show anyway? This is the first question that you need to ask yourself when you are contemplating attending a show as an exhibitor. In particular, it is a very useful question to ask at the beginning of a planning meeting. You may want to review this section when you meet with your planning team six months before the show, and use it as a basis for discussion. It focuses everyone on the reason for being at the show and can sort out the useful from the less useful reasons.

For most companies, I would argue that the *only* reason that can be justified as a business decision for going into a show is to sell your goods and services at a profit. It is easy to get distracted by peripheral reasons. These may be legitimate as *additional* reasons, but they should not over-shadow the main reason. Exhibiting is marketing. It is literally taking your goods to market. And when you take your goods to market, you expect to sell them for a profit.

Let us examine some of the common reasons for exhibiting, good and bad, that I have heard over the years:

*'We are going into the show because we do good business there / it's easier to sell at an exhibition / there are lots of buyers there.'* These are the best reasons of all. Depending on what research you look at, it is anything

from three to five times easier to sell at an exhibition than through cold calls and, consequently, it is substantially cheaper too.

There is nothing magical about this fact. A number of factors contribute to it, but the most important one is that a high proportion of show visitors are buyers. They come to the show with a need in mind, do enough comparison shopping to satisfy themselves that they are making a good decision and then they make a purchase, either at the show or, more often, after it.

*'We go to the show in order to get leads.'* Another excellent reason. In fact, for companies that have very successful shows, this is often the primary reason. Many companies make few or no sales at the show itself, and they do their selling afterwards to the people they met there. The gathering of leads is their principal function at a show.

One of the main focuses of this book is on gathering and following up leads.

*'We go to the show in order to demonstrate our products and services to people who are hard to get to.'* This may be a great reason for going into a show. Potential clients can be hard to meet for a number of reasons. They may be out of your normal territory or in a territory for which you do not have good coverage. They may be widely scattered. They may work in remote areas. Or they may be senior people who are hard to reach for all the usual reasons.

In chapters 4 and 5, there is more information on how you can maximise your chances of meeting with these people by contacting them before the show to invite them to your stand.

*'We want to use the show to introduce/launch a new product/service.'* This can be a very good way of getting fast market penetration for a new product. It will have good exposure because of the great number of people who will see it and to whom you may be able to demonstrate it.

However, you still have to do your research to ensure that sufficient numbers of your target market are going to be at the show. Additionally, you need to ensure that you can meet delivery requests if the product is very successful.

Bear in mind that, in the end, your aim is to sell your product, and you should assess a show for the launch of a new product as you would for your existing products: are we going to sell enough to justify the expense?

*'We want to get into a new market / to test a product in a new market / to get familiar with a new market, etc.'* This is similar to launching a new

product. After all, in a new market all your products are new. The ultimate aim is still to sell product, and the same rules apply: assess the show.

*'We want to get exposure.'* Exposure is an important part of marketing, and a show may be a great place to be seen, as there can be so many potential clients and influencers there if it is the right show for you.

But an exhibition is expensive. How much exposure are you going to get? To put it bluntly, how much is the exposure worth in sales? Can you measure it? Can you do a return-on-investment analysis on it?

The real question is: *Is exposure incompatible with making sales?* Can you do both? I am not arguing against exposure, but if it is the *only* reason for going into the show, you may be throwing away a great deal of business.

*'We want to let people personally try our products / to have our experts demonstrate them so that they are seen in the best light / to show equipment that cannot be taken to a sales call.'* These are excellent reasons for going into a show. One of the main advantages of exhibitions is precisely the opportunity to demonstrate your product and, in particular, to have clients try it themselves. There is more information further on about how to demonstrate your product to advantage.

However, you still have to do an analysis of the show to determine if it is worthwhile going into.

*'We want to send in new staff so they can get a feel for the industry.'* Bad idea. A show is not a place to train staff. Your company is on the line there, being judged. A very common complaint of exhibition visitors is that stand staff do not know what they are talking about. Do you want to come across as incompetent?

Train your staff thoroughly *before* the show and, in addition, have specialists on the stand if the regulars are likely to get asked questions they can't answer. See Chapter 7, *Two weeks before the show*, for more detailed information on the importance of training your staff in product knowledge— not only of your own products, but of your competitors' as well.

*'We want to see what our competitors are up to.'* While the fact that your competitors are exhibiting may be a good indication that the show is suitable for you, their presence by itself is not enough of a reason for you to attend. What if they are there for the wrong reasons? Are they making money out of the show? Ask yourself: Is this show right for *us*? And don't guess it, assess it.

As far as seeing what the competition is up to, a show *can* be a great place to check them out at close range. But if this is *all* you want to do, why not just attend as a visitor? Besides, there are lots of other ways of finding out what the competition is up to.

To sum up, checking out the competition is good, in fact I highly recommend it, but it should be a bonus to the successful marketing of your product.

*'People will wonder why we are not there. / Everyone else is there.'* At shows one does hear statements like: 'Such-and-such is not at the show. Maybe they're in trouble.' You may have made a comment like that yourself. What does it mean? Who will wonder if you are not there? Your customers? Your potential customers? Industry people? Your opposition?

Will your customers really abandon you if you are not at a particular show? Will people who might have done business with you shy away now? If you are a major player in your industry, your image is important, but if you are a small business, are prospective buyers even going to notice?

Everyone else is there? Good! It is probably an excellent show for you. Go into a show for positive reasons, intending to make sales, not out of fear.

*'If we don't go, we will miss out on a lot of potential business.'* You may very well be right. Exhibitions can be a most effective part of your marketing mix. But is *this* show right for you? If the business it brings in costs you more to get than it is worth, is attending the show good business?

*'We went last year. / We go every year.'* Did you make money last year?

*'We're going because we want to do market research for the potential introduction of a new product / to test or get to know a new market / to research attitudes to existing products.'* An exhibition can be a great place for getting feedback, as it is full of specialists in your field, including your existing and prospective clients. Not only can you show a new product to see if it is acceptable to the market—you can get a lot of feedback as to what features are considered important. And you can finetune a marketing strategy, trying different pricing points and marketing approaches to determine what sells best.

Depending on the nature of the product, to get maximum impact display it prominently on the aisle with a sign describing it as a new product.

However, you need to prepare for this activity if you want to obtain the best results. Make sure that you have determined ahead of time exactly what you want to know, and that you have trained and rehearsed your staff to elicit this information from people. You will also need a pre-designed form on which to record responses.

It is a two-step process: first, you interview stand visitors to determine if they are your target market and, second, you record their responses to the interview questions, along with any additional comments. This latter point is important. Some of the most valuable information you will get is likely to come from unsolicited comment. Be sure your staff prompt your visitor. 'Is there anything else that comes to mind?' Make room on your form for these responses.

Do not think of this method as a cheap and easy option. You still have to present your company professionally with your stand; your staff still have to be well-presented and trained. People will be judging not only your new product, but your whole company in the light of how they perceive your presence.

If you have a professional, attractive stand and well-presented, informed staff, that will reflect on the perceived quality and credibility of your product. If, on the other hand, you look like you threw your stand together in a hurry in your backyard and your staff are not a credit to you, you may come across like a backyard operator.

Finally, consider competitors. Many people go to shows to see what is new in the way of ideas. If your product is still in prototype stage, you may be exposing your great new idea to someone who is in a position to capitalise on it fast, thus cutting short your lead time in the market. Consider private viewings in a hospitality suite, to which you invite selected people.

*'We want to sell to other exhibitors.'* This may work, but do some research first. Get a list of exhibitors from the exhibition organiser and check the number of companies that are potential clients for you. If possible, visit the show. But be prepared to get short shrift from some of the other exhibitors. Like you, they are there to sell and may not appreciate your wasting their valuable time. You would probably feel the same about someone trying to sell to you while you were trying to sell to *your* potential clients. In fact, later in the book I discuss how to get rid of those very kinds of people.

If you do it, approach other exhibitors when they are not busy. Consider making an appointment to see them before the show opens in the morning or after it closes in the evening or during their breaks.

Treat these people as you would a show visitor. Qualify them. Make sure you speak to the right person, the decision-maker who would be purchasing your product. Do not rely on the person with whom you speak to pass the information on. Not many companies have a system for following up on the leads they get for *themselves*, let alone passing on leads for others. If the person to whom you should talk is not there, get the name and get in touch later.

Check with the organiser. Some have rules against canvassing, and all of them have rules against canvassing by non-exhibitors, for obvious reasons.

*'We're going to keep up with what's happening in the industry / to keep up with new developments / go to the seminars and lectures / talk to the experts / network / meet up with colleagues / attend functions / educate our staff.'* The seminars that often accompany trade shows can be very valuable. Not only are they educational in themselves, but they can be excellent networking opportunities: you can meet people there who will be valuable to you personally and to your business.

However, unless you are also going to set up a stand and market your goods at a profit, consider the option of just going to the show as a visitor. It will be much cheaper, easier and more pleasant.

*'We have to go into the show to fly the flag.'* I have heard this statement many times, and I have a standard response: 'Excellent! We can hire a small stand, put your company logo on a flag, put the flag on a pole and set up a big industrial fan to make it flutter. You do not even have to be there. It will be the talk of the show! Everyone will know that you went to the show and flew the flag!' I have never had anyone take me up on this offer, even though I think it would work a treat.

What does 'to fly the flag' actually mean? To maintain the company's profile? In whose eyes? Who are you flying the flag for? What is it actually going to achieve for you? And how much is it costing to fly the flag?

Nevertheless, there are times when this kind of activity can be justified. For example, if your company is a manufacturer, but has no retail outlets, you might want to be there to support your retailers. Or, if your company has gone through a difficult period, you might want to be there to assure customers and the industry that you are still standing. Or, indeed, if you are an industry leader, you may need to be there.

And sometimes it is important to fly the flag for personal reasons. 'Man does not live by bread alone' and, for some people, their business is their lifestyle.

But can you fly the flag *and* sell the product?

*'We go to make money.'* Good reason.

*'We're going to maintain public and customer relations.'* On occasion, a company decides, as part of its attendance, to send to the show some of their people, whether they be salespeople, senior management, technical and

R&D staff or various support staff, in order to give them the opportunity to meet customers (actual and potential) face to face. The rationale is that it will promote greater understanding between staff and customers, help to enhance company culture and ultimately improve the level of service given by the staff.

Perhaps it will. But there is a great danger in having untrained and uninformed staff on your stand. They will meet some of your existing clients, but they will meet many more people who are potential new clients. As I have pointed out before, one of the biggest complaints that show visitors have is that the staff on stands do not know the products and services being sold. Your image and your credibility are on show.

Ensure that *everyone* you put on your stand is thoroughly trained in both your product and in how to handle show visitors. Anyone who goes onto your stand should go through the same training processes as your dedicated stand staff. The importance of staff training cannot be overestimated and is discussed in more detail in Chapter 7.

*'We intend to entertain important customers and clients.'* Entertaining clients and customers works to strengthen relationships and is good business, of course. But if it is the *only* or *main* reason for going, why not just take a hospitality suite or book a permanent table at a good restaurant, get in touch with your clients and tell them you are going to use the money you're saving from the exhibition to show them an especially good time?

Again, I ask the question: is entertaining clients incompatible with making money?

*'We attend to meet existing clients and customers.'* Sometimes, if clients are widely dispersed or are in remote areas that are time-consuming and expensive to get to, an exhibition is a cost-effective way of making sales calls. But be careful not to focus just on existing clients while passing up a great opportunity to get new ones.

If the show is in an area where you already service your customers well, think carefully about the value of making a sale to an existing customer. Would you have made that sale anyway, only perhaps a bit later?

If you are running a 'show special'—offering extra product or giving a discount to entice people onto your stand—and your existing customers take advantage of it, then isn't this money that you have forgone that you would otherwise have received? By rights you should add this loss to your exhibition budget as a cost.

Always bear in mind that an exhibition is a marketing expense that will generally only be recouped via new or increased sales. It is at its most valuable when it is used to get new clients. The exception is when you want to up-sell or cross-sell to your existing customers. That is, when you want to upgrade them into newer versions of existing products they have already bought or when you want to sell them new products.

*'We go to shows to support the industry.'* Sometimes this is important, as we live in a political and social, as well as a business world. But how much is it costing you to support the industry? Is there any reason you cannot support the industry *and* make a profit as well?

In summary, I am clearly arguing that the main reason for going into shows is to grow your business. Most of the reasons outlined above for going into a show are good reasons as long as they are not the main ones but are only used in addition to the real justification, which is to make sales to new customers and clients.

# Choosing and assessing a show

Most of the time, choosing a show is not particularly difficult. Virtually every company can find mainstream, well-organised shows that service their industry well and provide a sufficient stream of potential clients to make it worthwhile. They are generally run by professional organisers with a track record of many successful shows.

With these mainstream shows the success or failure of an exhibitor is generally more dependent on the ability of the exhibitor than the organiser. This has been proved many times by the dramatic improvement in results that has come about when an exhibitor has instituted a good, properly managed exhibition strategy. It is sometimes startling how, after years of going into the same show with the same results, a company makes a massive improvement over just one show.

The decision whether to participate or not is harder when a company starts to consider smaller shows or ones that have been newly launched. In those situations one has to proceed more cautiously. Here are some guidelines:

## The bottom line: how many individuals representing your target market will be there?

With any show, whether it be new or established, a company has to assess the fit between their product or service and the show visitors. Since, as we discussed above, the central reason for going into a show is to sell your product, you need to decide if it is a profitable selling environment. The key piece of information to find out is how many potential customers will be at the show for you to talk to.

We are talking about an actual number of people. The total number of show visitors or a percentage of show visitors may both be misleading.

For instance, it is of no value to you that there are 50,000 visitors going through a show if none of them are buyers for your product or service. On the other hand, a very small show may be worthwhile. Many exhibitors do well at exhibitions sometimes having less than a dozen exhibitors, attached to small, specialised conferences, because virtually every attendee is a potential client, and the potential purchases are large.

When one speaks of percentages, if your target market makes up 1% of attendees at a small show, it may not be enough to justify your attendance, while 1% at a large show may present you with more potential clients than you can possibly handle.

So the prime question when considering attendance at a show must always be: 'How many individuals representing our target market will be there?'

## 'Who, exactly, do you want to talk to?'

It is important to be very precise about who, exactly, you want to talk to at each particular show. Who are you targeting as part of your business strategy? What is the target market that you are after? What kind of company is it? Specifically, what is the position (in their company) of the person you want your salespeople to talk to? In addition, this may change from show to show.

As an example, suppose you are an adhesives manufacturer and you are considering two woodworking shows at which to market your range of timber glues. One has an attendance of 2,000 and the other of 5,000. You are currently targeting small joineries which employ between six and twenty carpenters, as you find that these are the most profitable for you. You want to talk to the buyers and central influencers, who are generally the owners or the shop foremen.

So you ask the show organisers, 'How many owners and shop foremen of small timber workshops employing between six and twenty carpenters visit your show?'

The first organiser goes to her electronic database, does a search based on the questionnaires show visitors completed when they registered and tells you, 'We had 357 last year'. The second organiser tells you that his show mainly attracts hobbyists and artists/craftsmen, along with members of the general public who have an interest in handcrafted timber furniture.

Clearly you exhibit in the first show, even though it has a smaller total number of visitors, because it will have a great number of people that you want to talk to.

Bear in mind, however, that you still have to do a resources analysis in order to determine if that is enough visitors to make it worth your while, and if you have the resources to capitalise on the show. Some guidelines on doing that are outlined below.

## Smaller shows and new shows

What if you cannot find out the numbers of your target market that will be at the show, because the organiser does not have that kind of detail? Then you need to proceed along different lines. The most important factors are the history of the show and the track record of the organiser.

### The organiser

This should be your first point of call. Organisers often have a great deal of useful information that they will make available to you on request. Don't be afraid to grill them. Professional organisers are happy to work with potential clients to try to ensure that a show is a good fit for them as for exhibitors.

Ask them not only about the show, but about themselves. Do they have a track record of running successful shows? How many? What are they? Can you visit them? Ask for a list of previous and intending exhibitors so that you can contact them. Don't rely on a short list that the organiser may offer you. Ask for the complete list, so that you can contact those of your choice.

You should expect an organiser to be open with information. Trust your gut instinct. If it doesn't feel right, walk away. You'll survive without this show.

### The history of the show

How long has it been running? How many people attend? How accurate is this figure? Is it compiled by the organiser or independently? Does it include exhibitors? Does it count multiple entries (individuals going in and out of the show more than once) or unique visitors? Is there a demographic breakdown of visitors?

Ask the organiser, and regular exhibitors if you ring them, how the show has changed over the past two or three years. Shows have a life cycle: they may be growing, on a plateau or in decline.

Sometimes this is industry-driven. We saw this with home computer shows: they grew rapidly, with huge budgets being spent by exhibitors, and then went into decline, only to be replaced by network and IT shows as the big growth area. At other times a show may be going into decline because a competitor is taking over its market (in which case the competitor is in a growth phase). The switch can happen comparatively quickly, over a few years; one major exhibitor makes the move and is rapidly followed by others. A decline may also happen because of new management that is not competent. Equally, a show that was on a plateau or going into decline may be revitalised by new management.

The focus of the show may have changed, as the organisers change the people they are trying to attract, or broaden the base of attendees in order to keep pace with changes in the marketplace. These kinds of patterns may be useful to you or not, depending on your own focus.

## The show program

Read the literature carefully. Who is the show really targeting, with respect to both exhibitors and visitors? Try to get an overall feel for the show by considering the exhibitors, their products and their markets. Is there a good representation of companies that sell to your target market? If there is, it suggests that your target market attends.

What is the seminar schedule? Is it a quality program? What is the reputation of the speakers? Will that influence attendees? Would it influence *you* to go to the show? A strong program with important speakers suggests that the show is taken seriously and has credibility. This in turn adds to its credibility for visitors.

## Visit the show

Go on the last day if you can. Look at the general mood of the show. Do the exhibitors look energised, excited and happy, or is it a picture of gloom and depression? Ask exhibitors how it went for them. Tell them that you are thinking of exhibiting at the next show. They will generally be very open with you. Bear in mind, however, that the response you get from individual exhibitors may be determined by factors outside the control of the organiser and, in any case, may have little bearing on how good the show may be for you.

Some exhibitors will tell you that it is a bad show, but the reasons may be that they didn't know what they were doing, had unattractive or inappropriate products or badly trained staff. Others will tell you that it was a great show, but their criteria for success may be different from yours or your target markets may be different.

You may be able to get better information by talking to those exhibitors whose customers are the same as yours (even though they may be selling different products), and focusing your questions specifically on the number and quality of visitors that were useful to them.

### Ask your clients
Make a representative list of your clients and potential clients and ring them. Tell them that you are considering going into the show as an exhibitor and ask them if they visit it. If you speak to a statistically significant number, you should end up with a fair idea of how many potential clients you could expect to see there. While you're at it, ask them what other shows they go to through the year.

### Ask your competitors
If you are on good terms with any competitors who go into the show, ring them and ask if it is a good show. Of course, if they are on the ball and it *is* a good show, they are likely to tell you it is terrible!

### Ask companies that target your clients
From the list the organisers have given you, choose companies that target the same people you do, even though they may not sell the same products, and ask their opinion of the show.

## Assessing a show you have attended previously
Thinking about a show in which you have participated before? Trying to decide if it is worth going into again? The central question is: *Was the show profitable?*

Some companies find this hard to quantify. Most know how much they spent on a particular show, or can work it out if they have an overall exhibition budget that covers more than just one show. But they sometimes have trouble determining just how much they got back for their investment of time and money.

If this is your situation, have a look at the section on doing a return-on-investment analysis of a show in Chapter 14.

# Choosing a stand position

The earlier you book a stand in a show, the wider your choice. For some shows that are in great demand, it is vital to book early in order to get a good stand. In some long-established and important shows, the same premium areas are held for years by the same companies.

Some organisers have facilities at the show itself for booking the next year's stand, and may even come around and ask you.

There are two basic factors to consider in choosing a stand: size and position. The biggest factor determining the size of the stand is your budget. The second factor is the size of your equipment and display and the third is the number of your stand staff. The three are interrelated. More salespeople generally mean more leads. But more salespeople also mean a larger stand and hence a bigger budget.

As a guide, each salesperson needs about four square metres of clear floor space that is not taken up by displays and equipment. That is the personal space needed by one stand staffer and one or two visitors. You can squeeze that a bit with bigger stands, especially if you have corner, peninsula or island stands.

As to position, generally it does not matter much where your stand is because traffic will flow throughout a show if it is well laid out. The exception is gloomy areas and dead ends, but even then you can somewhat overcome those factors by making your stand a blaze of light and having something interesting going on.

Regarding types of stands, a *standard* stand has three walls and one open side; a *corner* stand is on a corner and has two walls and two open sides; a *peninsula* stand has one wall and three open sides; and an *island* stand is open all round. There are also variations in the form of L-shaped stands, and so on.

Usually, the more open sides you have, the better. It makes your stand more open and inviting to come onto, it gives you more frontage along which to attract visitors, and it makes your stand appear bigger. It also effectively increases its size as you can spill out into the aisles more readily. And, finally, it allows your stand to be seen more often because you are on more crossroads.

While these advantages of corner stands are reflected in the greater prices that organisers generally charge for them, each company's exhibition needs are different, and stands need to be chosen according to what is intended to be done on them. For instance, one company might need a lot of wall space.

# It sounds all right, but will I make money?—a resources analysis

After you have decided that a show has a goodly number of your target market visiting it, there is one more necessary step. Ask yourself: can I make a profit on this marketing investment?

Most companies start with a budget. They decide at some stage how much they will spend on a show. The following chapter, *Six months before the show*, takes a detailed look at budgeting, but for now we will do a rough calculation to see whether we have the resources to take advantage of a particular show.

Let us suppose your company budgets $20,000. How many sales do they need to make a good return on that investment? Let's run some speculative figures. Yours will, of course, be different.

The organiser tells you that there will be 3,500 visitors to the show, but your research tells you that only about 450 of those will be potential buyers for you. However, you will not speak to all of those. Let's say that in their wanderings (and with some help from you through pre-show invitations and publicity) two thirds of them end up on your stand. That's 300.

Can you interview that many people? It would seem so, because you have three people on the stand, each talking to an average of six people per hour for the 24 hours that the show is open in total. That's 432. Plenty to manage the 300. But wait. There will be others who stop at your stand as well. Let's say that only one in five of the people you talk to will actually be a potential client. That's 20% of 432, which equals 86.

You talk to these 86, record their details, follow them up in a timely fashion after the show and you sell to about one in three. That's 28 new customers. It doesn't sound like much from 3500 attendees, but let's look at the figures.

Let's say that an initial sale to a new client averages out at $1500. Those 28 sales then total $42,000. But there is one more step. You need to take into account the lifetime value of your clients. That value is the average of the total amount that all your clients spend with you from the first sale to the last that you make to them.

Suppose the lifetime value of your clients is $10,000. Those 28 sales, therefore, represent $280,000 eventually, which you may consider a fair return on your $20,000 marketing dollar.

It is important to remember that these are hypothetical figures and not based on a real show. Your own figures will be different, because all the factors will be different—number of potential clients, number of staff, hours of operation, closing ratios, dollar amounts. There is no formula. It always has to be worked out on a company-by-company and show-by-show basis.

Bear in mind, too, that you can swing the odds greatly in your favour by taking a strategic approach and by training your staff. This can multiply your results many times over and transform your exhibition results.

However, the above example gives you some rule-of-thumb guidance on how to decide whether to go into a show. But, in the end, the only way you can ever really assess a show's success is by doing a return-on-investment calculation after the show, when all the figures are in. Again, that is covered in more detail in Chapter 14.

Chapter 3

# Six months before the show

- Meet with the exhibition management team to plan the show
- Review the previous show
- Set a target for the coming show
- Prepare a budget
- Decide what you will display
- Decide on your stand approach
- Decide on promotional activity
- Dressing for the show
- Go through the exhibitor manual
- Prepare a written action plan

# Meet with the exhibition management team to plan the show

In the previous chapter, *Twelve months before the show*, we assessed and chose the show, and booked a space. Now, six months before the show, is a good time to meet with the exhibition management team and begin working on it. Your team may be a team of one—yourself—or it may involve others.

This is a planning meeting, and it should include all those who are involved in the logistics of getting the show together, but not necessarily the staff who are going to be on the stand, or support staff. There will be other meetings involving them.

The purpose of this meeting is to plan the show and decide what has to be done, who will do it, and when. What follows are the areas to be addressed. Not all of them may be relevant to you, however.

# Review the previous show

You may want to begin by reviewing the results of a previous show, whether it be the predecessor of the one you are now planning, or simply a show you have been in previously.

## Did we make money?

You can do a return-on-investment analysis if you have measured key indicators and kept records. An ROI analysis is the only way to accurately measure the results of exhibiting and determine whether a show is worth going into again.

Details of how to go about doing such an analysis can be found in Chapter 14.

## How did our stand perform?

How did the stand look? Did it convey the image of our company that we wanted to communicate? Was it inviting for people to come onto it? How did it stop people in the aisle? Was it big enough? Was it big enough during busy periods? How did it effectively sell our product or service to visitors who were unattended while we were all busy? How was the position? Was there a good traffic flow past it?

How can we improve it next time?

## Literature
Budget for brochures and other support material for the show; include the cost of any of the normal brochures that you use, as well as the design and printing of material you produce specially for the show, including lead forms.

## Transport
Delivery of goods to and from the stand and your premises, couriers, etc. constitute your transport costs.

## Consumables
This item includes samples, giveaways, consumables for demonstrations.

## Venue costs
Here we have rigging, telephone, fax and data lines, water, waste, compressed air, etc.

## Advertising and promotion
Under this budget item come pre-show mail-out campaigns (including purchase of contact lists), press kit preparation and dissemination, competition prizes, advertising in trade magazines.

## Post-show follow-up
This stage may involve the cost of telemarketing services, database software, temporary staff for recording leads, fulfilment of post-show packages, and mail-outs.

## Client entertainment
This item may include dinners, drinks, gifts, or a hospitality suite.

## Show events
An exhibition dinner, cocktail party, seminars, and staff registrations are the usual things to be included here.

## Other/contingency
There are nearly always costs associated with an exhibition that one has not foreseen and budgeted for. Allow 10% of your total budget.

## Juggling the budget

Most companies have a show budget within which the show manager has to do the best he or she can. It can be a bit of a juggling act. The budget, stand size and staffing levels are closely related: change one and you change the others.

The place to start is your budget. It tells you how much business you need to write to make the show profitable. Now you can work out how many sales you need to make and thus how many leads you have to generate (if you know your conversion ratios). Once you have the number of leads, you can also work out how many people you need on the stand in order to generate those leads. The number of staff will, in turn, influence the size of your stand.

That may all sound a bit complicated. Perhaps we can make it clearer by taking the example we used earlier when we assessed the show for suitability. Remember, this is only a very simple example. Real life is more complex. The more your figures are based on past shows, the more accurate your planning will be.

We calculated earlier that we would have three people on the stand, that they would get 86 strong leads and that this would result in 28 sales, worth $42,000 in immediate sales and $280,000 in long-term sales, when the lifetime value of customers is taken into account.

You have a budget of $20,000 for the show. You do some preliminary rough costing:

| | |
|---|---|
| The space: | $6,000 |
| The stand: | $5,000 |
| Show services: | $1,500 |
| Direct staff costs (wages): | $3,600 |
| Advertising and promotion: | $3,500 |
| Entertainment: | $1,500 |
| Post-show follow-up: | $1,500 |
| Contingency (10%): | $2,260 |
| TOTAL | $24,860 |

Hmm, blown the budget already . . . what can we take out? It is important, when cutting a budget, to take out those items which will not affect the number of qualified leads you get.

The stand space? We have a 6-metre by 3-metre stand, two standard modules. We could cut it down to a single module, 3 × 3, but that would not give us enough space for three staff. A 3 × 3 stand can really only take two people. And there would not be enough room for all the equipment we want to display. So that has to stay.

The stand? This is our corporate stand, and it is an integral part of the image we want to project. It also displays our product to its best advantage. That cost represents the complete installation and dismantling, including lighting and power, because our exhibition contractor does it all. It also includes the amortised costs of its construction. That should stay.

Show services? A large part of that is the rigging for hanging the new banners above the stand. If we eliminate this item, we also do not have to produce the new banners. That saves us $1,200.

Staff costs? We have to have three people on the stand; otherwise, we will get a third fewer leads and a third fewer sales, dropping the figure to 18. We have to keep our three people. Anyway, staff costs are already under-estimated.

Advertising and promotion? We have to have the literature, and the pre-show mail-out, since that is specifically targeting the people we want to reach, and will drive more traffic to our stand. But we can probably do away with the advertising in the trade press. That saves us $2,500.

Entertainment? We will be taking some clients out to lunch and dinner but, on close examination, that figure is perhaps a bit generous. We can save $900 there.

Post-show follow-up? We absolutely have to keep that. Without it we will not be able to follow up properly, which will directly affect sales.

Contingency? We need that item but, with the reduced budget, it comes down.

The budget now reads:

| | |
|---|---|
| The space: | $6,000 |
| The stand: | $5,000 |
| Show services: | $ 300 |
| Direct staff costs (wages): | $3,600 |
| Advertising and promotion: | $1,000 |
| Entertainment: | $ 600 |
| Post-show follow-up: | $1,500 |
| Contingency (10%): | $1,800 |
| TOTAL | $19,800 |

Ah, if only real life were so neat! But you get the idea . . .

# Decide what you will display

What will you display? How will you do it? What resources will you need to make it happen? Resources include both physical resources and staff.

## Allocation of resources

You will need to decide how much product to have on the stand and how to show it to its best advantage. Generally speaking, simpler is better. For instance, it may be more effective to have only representative samples of your product on the stand, with the whole range illustrated in catalogues. If you are doing a physical demonstration, you may also need to have equipment and consumables.

The best way of promoting your products and services on a stand is through a demonstration, as was outlined in the previous chapter. This is a *show*, after all. If your product or service is difficult to demonstrate, find a way, even if it is just someone talking to a video or PowerPoint presentation.

A stand contractor or designer will be able to advise you on the best way of displaying your product. And you can find more information on how to demonstrate your product in Chapter 7.

As to staff, if you are a small company, you may not have much of a choice about numbers. Anyone who can be spared will be on the stand.

While more staff generally means more leads, it is best not to crowd your stand as a stand that is too crowded will discourage visitors. If you want to have more staff, then you should get a bigger stand. However, this will not only add to space costs, but may add to stand dressing costs too.

# Decide on your stand approach

## Types of stand construction

There are several degrees to which you can get involved in the building of your stand, from doing it all yourself right up to getting a contractor to design and build you a custom stand.

### A standard or 'shell scheme' stand

This is the entry-level stand. A 'shell scheme' is the standard booth usually offered by the organiser as part of the show. Such stands are generally built in blocks consisting of 'modules' or 'booths', with a floor area measuring 3 metres by 3 metres.

Most are constructed of 'system': lengths of grooved aluminium that are locked together to form walls and fascias. The wall panels come in a variety of materials and colours. The 'fascia' is a kind of board or pelmet running around the open perimeter of the stand, above head level, and supporting a sign for the exhibiting company's name.

Some kind of carpeting is usually provided and often the stand comes with some basic lighting and a power point.

This is the most inexpensive way to get a stand, and it serves the purposes of many companies very well after they have dressed it up with some furniture and their product and display materials.

## Two simple techniques to improve a shell scheme stand

If you have hired a standard shell scheme stand from the organiser, there are two simple and inexpensive things you can do to improve it: remove the fascia and increase the lighting.

Removing the fascia immediately opens up your stand, making it seem bigger and more inviting to walk onto. And this improvement won't cost you anything.

On the form you find in your exhibitor manual, on which you are to specify the name you want to appear on the fascia, you may request that the fascia not be put up. You may want to add that you still require the fascia *signs*, which you can affix to the walls of your stand, though I would highly recommend improving your image by having good-quality signs made of your company name and logo. Have them put on a hard backing and you can use them in show after show.

The second improvement you can make is to increase the amount of lighting on the stand. Some lights are a standard part of your shell scheme stand. These are usually hung on a rail behind your fascia. Since you no longer have a fascia, you will have to specify lights on arms. These are lights on rods or short poles that are fixed to the top of the stand walls and angled back to shine onto them. You may find them listed on the electricity order form in your exhibitor manual. If not, you will have to ask for them.

You need to have enough lights to brightly light up the whole length of your stand wall. As a rule of thumb, a 150-watt light will illuminate a one-metre wall panel, but ask the advice of the electrician, especially when it comes to larger floodlights or low-voltage lights.

The improved lighting may cost some hundreds of dollars, depending on the size of your stand, but it is worth it for the way it will make your stand shine.

## A custom stand

At the other end of the extreme to a shell scheme stand is a custom stand and, if you can afford it, it pays to get one built. A custom stand is one that is expressly designed and built for your company. The advantages are that it allows you to project exactly the sort of image you want, it can display your equipment to maximum effect, it can make you stand out from the rest of the exhibiting crowd and can leave the show visitors with a positive and memorable image of you.

However, a custom stand is expensive. You will need to determine how much you are going to spend on it before you brief the stand contractor; he will have to know your budget before he can begin designing it.

If you do not have a contractor, brief three, assess their designs, and choose one.

## A system stand

A less expensive way of achieving a custom stand look is by having a 'system' stand built. As mentioned earlier, 'system' is the aluminium-framed panelling system that is used to build standard shell stands, but it can be configured into a variety of towers, plinths, benches and wall types. It can be further customised via coloured and painted panels, graphics, light boxes, banners and so on. A system stand can look very impressive in the hands of a good designer.

The cost advantage of a system stand over a fully custom-built stand is that you only *hire* it from the contractor, rather than buy it.

## A professionally dressed stand

A less expensive way still of getting a unique look is to hire the standard 'shell scheme' provided by the organiser and then hire someone to 'dress' or decorate it, including advising you on how to display your products or services.

A stand dresser is a specialist, akin to a window dresser who, for a comparatively modest fee, will make your stand look much more pro-fessional. The contractor who is providing the shell scheme for the show often handles this service, too. Otherwise, the show catalogue will usually recommend one or more companies.

## A DIY stand

The least expensive option of all is to do it yourself. However, when you factor in your own time, it may turn out to be more expensive than you think. But if it is a matter of cash flow—as it often is—the DIY choice is understandable.

The drawback with this approach is that it can look unprofessional and reflect badly on your company. The appearance of your stand often influences the way show visitors perceive your products and service.

# Stand design

Good stand design is the result of both talent and years of experience. While experienced stand contractors can provide a great deal of good advice about what works and does not work in an exhibition context, below are some guidelines that may help you to get a better result whether you do the stand yourself or get someone to do it for you. They may also help you in assessing designs that are submitted to you.

There are three broad principles of stand design:

1. The stand has to be seen from a distance.
2. It has to stop people in the aisle.
3. It has to work as a selling tool.

## The stand has to be seen from a distance

Banners and towers are the two common ways to achieve this. Banners are generally suspended above the stand from the ceiling of the exhibition venue, and need the services of riggers to get them into place. Both banners and towers can be made more noticeable by illuminating them with flood-lights. Always incorporate some type of lighting with your towers and banners to maximise their effect.

A company may decide to use them in order to raise the company profile and have as many people see its name as possible. If it is a market leader, it may want to project and reinforce that 'leader image' by giving an impression of size and dominance.

Banners and towers also help people find you. It can be easy to miss an individual company in a very large exhibition.

Apart from your name, you may find it useful to put a simple message up high, telling people what you are offering, especially if your company is not well known. It may be as simple a phrase as 'modems, faxes, copiers', or it may incorporate a marketing message or your company slogan, such as 'The fastest modems in the world!' or 'The printer the other printers use!' This kind of simple message appeals directly to your target market. Someone who is in the market for a modem or a printer will be more likely to move toward your stand.

## The stand has to stop people in the aisle

There is only a limited time at a show in which to attract visitors' attention, perhaps only three or four seconds. An exhibition is a very busy place, and visitors have many things vying for their attention as they are walking along the aisles. They generally scan each stand as they come up to it and if they see something of interest they will stop to have a closer look.

A stand, therefore, has to present its product in such a way that it is quickly and easily identified, and in a manner that is attractive to its target audience. Some of the main ways of enhancing the attractiveness of the presentation are outlined below. One of the most powerful, of course, is to demonstrate your product, and that is covered in detail later in the book.

## The stand has to work as a selling tool

An exhibition stand is an environment in which to present your product in the best possible light. You can do things you may not be able to do in a prospective client's office: you can set up demonstrations; you can run videos and show displaying graphics of the product in use; you can have a much broader range of your products on display than can be taken into the field by a salesperson. Perhaps most useful of all, prospective clients can have the hands-on experience of trying the product themselves.

In terms of a company 'selling itself', the look of the stand is very important. Show visitors will judge a company by its stand, especially if they do not know it. If it is important in business for a person to present well because first impressions count, it is equally true that a stand makes a first impression that colours the way a visitor will perceive your product and the service you are likely to provide.

If your stand looks professional and well organised, the visitor will be likely to assume that your company is, too. If, on the other hand, it looks as if it were knocked together in your backyard, the impression your visitor may have is that you yourself are something of a backyard operator.

A good-looking stand also helps to increase the morale of the people staffing it, and high morale will make them more effective.

## Some practical stand considerations
Let us now look at a range of more practical considerations that can be implemented in order to help make a stand perform at its maximum.

### Focus outward
Demonstrate on the aisle. The most effective place is at the edge of your stand. This allows interested visitors to stop in the neutral territory of the aisle, and watch from safety, without having to make the commitment of walking onto your stand.

Even one-to-one demonstrations, such as a PowerPoint presentation that is made after a visitor has been qualified as being genuinely interested, should be held close to the aisle and facing outwards. In this situation the monitor screen or, if you are using a laptop, a second screen, should be positioned above the heads of the presenter and visitor, so that passers-by can watch over their shoulders.

Product displays should also be positioned so that they can easily be seen from the aisle, rather than hidden away in the depths of the stand.

### Group products meaningfully
There is an enormous amount to see at a show, and visitors can easily get into a state of information overload, as a result of which they do not attend as sharply as they did at first. If someone is walking past your stand and all they see is a jumble of stuff, they are more likely to just give up and look to the next thing.

On an exhibition stand, less can be more. Keep your displays simple. A few representative examples of your products, well displayed, are all that is needed to draw interested visitors onto your stand.

If you do want to have a large number of your products on display, group them by displaying them on different-coloured display boards, or by framing them in some way. A descriptive sign at the top of each group can also help. This kind of grouping allows the eye to make sense of what it is seeing, because it first sees a simple pattern and can then zero in meaningfully on details.

## Lighting

In my opinion, virtually all exhibition stands are under-lit. Most stands can safely triple the amount of light they are using.

As human beings, we are are attracted to light. A brightly-lit stand looks much more cheerful and inviting than a gloomy one. Use floodlights to increase the overall level of illumination, and spotlights to draw the eye to important features, such as your equipment or special offers.

## Signage

Signs are one of the simplest and most powerful ways to get your message across. At their most basic, they tell visitors who you are. This, however, may not be very useful. We have probably all been to exhibitions and walked past stands, especially those that provide intangible services, without having any idea what the company is offering. The company name gives no clue to the services it provides. Visitors are hardly likely to walk up on the off-chance that it may be something of interest to them. They'll keep walking.

Use signs to tell people what you do and what you are offering.

There are three levels of signage, the *first* being signage that is seen from a distance. We addressed this type earlier. It is large signage, up high, that identifies your company and perhaps provides a simple message about what you are offering.

Once a visitor is close enough to see inside your stand, that signage has done its job and is not in the range of vision or of interest any longer.

*The second level of signage* is designed to be seen and read from the aisle. So it is big, simple and short enough to be read at a glance. It identifies what you do, and what you are offering.

The two most attention-grabbing words on an exhibition stand are *New!* and *Free!* Splash them big, bold and colourful, and you'll be sure to attract attention.

These large signs should offer benefits to your target market. Rather than put a sign on your machine that says 'The Megalith R357-2G', put one that says 'Increase your carton-sealing speeds by 30% and reduce downtime by 17%!' That should make your buyers want to come onto the stand to find out more!

Into this category also comes your company name and logo, which should be prominently displayed, and well-lit.

*The third level of signage* is up close and personal, and is designed to be read on an individual level by someone who is on the stand. We're talking here of such things as labels on equipment and listings of features or, better still, statements of the benefits that your equipment can provide. They should be easy to read quickly and may be in the form of bullet points on a wall or on a piece of equipment. Diagrams usually come under this heading, too.

These signs are not meant to replace the detailed explanations your staff are there to provide, but should augment, support and illustrate their statements and claims.

## Graphics

Graphics should be large and simple, able to be seen and understood from the aisle. The most useful role a graphic can play in an exhibition is to halt your target market in the aisle, and once it has done that, to draw them onto the stand.

As an example, if a company is selling fire-fighting chemicals, then one large image of an industrial fire being brought under control will be more easily recognised and understood by fire officers than lots of little photographs that cannot be properly seen from the aisle.

## Preparing a brief for a stand contractor

If you are having a stand built, the designer is the most important person in the creation process. He or she is the one who actually decides how the stand is going to look and how it will be laid out.

It is unusual for an exhibitor to meet directly with the designer. More often you will have the stand contractor's representative come to see you to discuss your stand. The representative will in turn brief the designer. What does the designer need to know? He or she will not have met you, probably will not know your company, and has to get an understanding of you from the representative and any additional material you provide. Provide as much information as you can. Below are some of the areas you need to cover.

### The show

In which show, or shows, is the stand to be used? The show itself will to some extent influence the design look. For instance, if you are selling your paints at an interior design show the stand design may be somewhat different from what it would be if you were selling them at a hardware suppliers' show.

## The venue

The venue can influence the design. For instance, there may be height restrictions in certain venues such as hotels, or in parts of exhibition halls. This can determine the height of walls and towers, the hanging of banners and the placement of lights.

## Your company details

You need to supply as much detail as you can about your company, in addition to the products and services that you offer. Brochures are very useful in this respect, as they allow the designer to get a feel for your company image and then design your stand to reflect it.

## The target audience

Who is your target market? Unless you want to brand your company very strongly, a design can be a balance between company image and appeal to the target market.

## A floor plan of the show and of your stand

A floor plan of the show allows the designer to see where your stand is positioned in the hall and make decisions about how it should be oriented to make the best use of traffic flow. The stand size and shape, including how many walls it has and where it is open to the aisles, will naturally influence basic design features.

## Staff numbers

The number of stand staff can influence other factors, including layout of equipment, configuration of displays and amount of bench space.

## Equipment to be displayed

How much equipment do you plan to have on the stand? How do you want to use it and display it? What access do you need? Do you need to walk around it or can it go against a wall? How should it be placed in relation to other equipment? What are its dimensions, footprint, height?

Provide pictures of your equipment if you can, so that the designer can get an idea of how it looks and position it to best advantage.

## Storage needs

How much storage do you need for brochures, equipment, consumables, personal effects, and so on? Having enough storage on a stand is vital, and it needs to be designed in.

## The budget

The designer needs to know your budget. It is almost impossible to start work without a budget. Preferably this should be a definite figure but, at the very least, a ball-park figure or a range.

Sometimes a person may feel that if he gives the contractor a definite budget, he will be taken advantage of in some way: the contractor will give him as little as he can get away with. However, most contractors, when they get a new brief, will assume that it is a competitive situation, with at least two other companies tendering, so they will try to do the best they can.

Designers will always try to maximise what they can give you within your budget, and a good designer is very clever about stretching your budget by using inexpensive methods to achieve great-looking results but, in the end, you get what you pay for.

## Image

Finally, what image do you intend to project? Is it fun and bubbly, stable and conservative, cutting edge or, as one company memorably told me, pretty much all of these combined?

It is important that you let the designer know, since good designers can, through the use of colour, shape, form and all the other tools at their disposal, generate the image you want people to have of you.

# Decide on promotional activity

Why promote? Some exhibitors resent the thought that they should do any promotion at all to attract people to their stand. *After all*, they say, *that's what I'm paying my money to the organiser for!* That may or may not be a sensible attitude, depending on circumstances. Some shows may have so many of your potential clients that you cannot possibly talk to them all. In that case, pre-show promotion makes no sense, but it may pay you to do some at-show promotion.

Most times, however, while it is true that a good show will deliver enough prospects to make attendance worthwhile for you, you can do a great deal yourself to increase the number and quality of visitors to your stand. This takes the form of pre-show promotion and at-show promotion. Do not confuse these promotions with company promotion itself; their sole purpose is to attract more traffic.

Pre-show promotion can attract people who were not intending to come to the show at all, as well as those who were intending to come but had not planned to seek you out. It also reinforces the intention of those who *were* planning to see you.

At-show promotion attracts people already at the show. You cannot assume that everyone will walk past your stand, especially if it is a big show. Some might inadvertently miss your particular section of aisle; others might run out of time before they have seen all the show. Many have only limited time to spend there. They plan ahead, deciding who they will visit and then, if they have time, they will look around to see what else catches their attention.

## Offer benefits

Remember that you need to make it worthwhile for the person you are contacting to come to the stand. You have to offer something of value to *them*. You need to offer *benefits*. The focus is on your target market, not, primarily, on your company, product or service.

Ideally, this benefit should be so compelling, it should arouse such interest and enthusiasm that, even if they were not planning to go to the show, they will now go just to visit you.

## Who is your target?

Your target market needs to be very precisely defined if you are to do pre-show and at-show promotion. Sometimes it is the same as your normal customer base but, at other times, it is more narrowly focused, as when you are promoting a particular product from your range, or offering a totally new product.

Who do you want to talk to? Who do you want to walk onto your stand? What is their position in the company? What sort of company is it? The more precise you are here, the more successful you will be in reaching the right people.

The question of defining your buyers is covered in more detail in Chapter 7.

## Visitor incentives

Some companies offer incentives of various kinds to entice visitors onto their stand. The best are those that offer the benefits of your product, as discussed above, because they are the most likely to attract those people who have a genuine interest in your particular product or service.

If you intend to offer incentives, bear in mind that many companies have strict rules as to the value of gifts their employees are allowed to accept, often limiting them to nominal amounts—some, including government departments, will not allow the acceptance of any gifts at all.

However, an incentive does not have to be something of monetary value, it can just as well be something of *perceived* value, such as a chance to meet a celebrity.

Why not give away information? One of the main reasons people go to shows is to educate themselves, to benefit by seminars, to keep up with what is happening in the industry. Information costs you virtually nothing to give away. In fact, along with a smile and a cold, it is one of the few things you can give away and still keep!

If you target your product's genuine buyers, and your invitation makes your offering sound interesting enough, even just the chance to see your new products may be incentive enough.

## Pre-show promotion

Pre-show promotion falls into four categories:

- Personal invitation
- Mail invitation
- Advertising and press releases
- Email

Only advertising and press releases will be addressed in this chapter, because they need to be planned well ahead. Personal and mail invitation, and email, are covered in Chapter 4, *Three months before the show*.

The most common forms of pre-show exhibition advertising are press releases, articles in trade magazines, advertising in trade magazines and hitchhiking a ride on your normal advertising.

## Press releases

Press releases are really a form of advertising. You are hoping that the media outlet you are sending your release to will print or show something about your product or service. The big advantage of this is that it is free.

Press releases need to be sent to publications that are read by your target market and, for most companies, that means a trade magazine servicing your industry.

The subject of a press release has to be newsworthy. Put yourself in the shoes of an editor. He or she will ask: Is this going to be of interest to my readers? If you have something interesting enough, it may even rate a feature article.

The reason you should start thinking about press releases now, six months before the show, is because magazines often have lead times of months, and you want to have your exposure in the months leading up to the show, not after it.

Press releases have a format that needs to be followed to be acceptable to editors. If you don't know what that is, there are a number of books that will enlighten you. Alternatively, you can hire a professional writer.

Many shows have media attending them. Find out from the organiser who is coming, and send a press release inviting them to come to your stand to see your newsworthy new product. If your product merits a photo opportunity or a video image, all the better.

## Advertising in trade magazines

Many shows have a trade magazine associated with them, and they often bring out a special show issue. If you do intend to advertise in these magazines, it may be more effective to spread your publicity over a number of issues leading up to the show, rather than put it all in the one issue that comes out during the show.

## Hitchhike a ride on your normal advertising and communication

You can make your normal advertising work double time by adding an invitation to visit you at the show. Even if your copy is already prepared, it is generally easy for your designer to add to it.

You can do the same with your letters by setting up a template on your word processor so that it prints an invitation to the show each time you print a letter. You can do a similar thing with your emails. You can also promote your presence at the show on your website, and by adding a sticker to your brochures.

## At-show promotion

As with pre-show promotion, the purpose is to attract people to your stand.

### Exhibition Catalogue listing

Most show guides have an exhibitor list that includes a short company profile. In the exhibitor manual that you get before the show, you will generally find a form for your submission.

Many show visitors read the guide during the show, especially when they sit and take a break. Instead of giving them a dry company profile, why not treat this message as advertising copy and draw visitors to your stand by offering exciting benefits?

### Exhibition Catalogue advertising

You can advertise in the show guide. Often this is a special edition of a trade magazine.

### Brochures

There is an old industry joke about brochures: Take only enough brochures for the first day. At the end of the day, go around to all the garbage bins, take out your brochures, and you'll have enough for the second day.

What proportion of brochures actually get read? Who knows? A good number would certainly get dumped or lost in the shuffle or are the victims of good intent.

So, should you give out brochures? I recommend that you have some on the stand for people to take away with them for those who have not attended for one reason or another. If one genuine buyer takes a brochure and it leads to a sale, that will hopefully more than cover the cost of the wasted ones.

People who are genuinely interested in your product should also be given one. Many of these people are collecting information so that they can later consider competing products and make a decision on which to buy. People who are part of a team that is researching a buying decision should definitely be given as much information as they need to decide to short-list your company.

On the other hand, if a person is clearly not a prospective client, don't waste your money.

But whatever you do, you should still send a brochure after the show, even to those people to whom you have already given one, along with your follow-up letter.

This serves several purposes. First, it puts your brochure in people's hands again, thus reminding them of you and reinforcing your message. Second, it allows your literature to be seen on its own, and not amongst your competition's literature. This makes you stand out. Third, because it comes soon after you spoke with the person and arrives with a personalised covering letter, it shows that you are professional and that you follow up as you say you will. This is a measure of your service, and it will make your prospective client more likely to do business with you. Finally, it gives you a reason for following up and a conversational opening. More on that in Chapter 11.

A final word. Your literature needs to look professional; it is the face of your company. Someone who looks at it after the show will judge you by it. If it looks scrappy and amateurish, they will think your company is like that. If it looks professional, they will think you are, too. Get it professionally designed and printed on good-quality paper.

The only circumstance in which you may be able to get away with cheap photocopied literature is if you are promoting a 'hot' show special and you want it to look as if it is a very temporary offer—so people will feel that if they do not buy now, they will miss out.

## Giveaways

In most cases if you are planning to hand out gimmicky giveaways, don't bother, save your money. They don't work.

Is a print works manager really going to be inspired to buy your printing paper because they have a leaky pen with your name on it somewhere in the bottom of their desk drawer? Is a hotel beverage manager really going to stock your wine on the basis of the corkscrew you gave to one of his chefs at a show?

Rather, aren't purchasing decisions made on a somewhat more hard-headed basis, involving meetings and discussions, and negotiations on price and terms?

Pens, rulers, stickers, badges, caps—all given away in the hope that the name of the company sitting there will somehow prompt someone to buy from it. But the purchasing clerks I've known have made their decisions on the basis of the people they like to deal with, on reliability and quality of product, and on price. And even then, they will often ring around to ascertain who has the best current deal.

But then again, you never can tell. The marketing manager of a large corporation producing abrasives had persuaded a visitor to his stand, the owner of a large factory, on the benefits of his abrasive products over the ones he was currently using. But he was having trouble getting him to make the commitment to switch by ordering his first batch of product. The man wanted to think about it.

It was a big initial order, and much bigger still when repeat orders were taken into account. Casting about for some other incentive to offer, the marketing manager picked up one of the coffee mugs they had on the stand as giveaways and made his final offer: 'Tell you what, if you make a decision now, I'll throw in this coffee mug for free.'

This was a 30-cent ceramic mug made in China, with the company's logo on it. The man looked at it, laughed, and said, 'All right, you've won me!'

The moral? Miracles can happen. Don't rely on miracles, however. Don't rely on giveaways. Rely on a properly planned and executed whole-of-show strategy.

Are there any kinds of giveaways that do work? Samples of your product may work. Give them to people to try and then use the trial to give you a reason to follow up and sell ongoing purchases. Software manufacturers and distributors know the value of this strategy. They distribute limited versions of their software, aware that a certain number of users will like the product enough to buy it.

## Show specials

Another kind of in-show promotion is a 'show special'. A show special is a giveaway. You are giving away money. Will people buy on the basis of the show special? Absolutely. They still have to be in the market, and you still have to sell the product to them, but everyone loves a bargain. Some companies even put off major capital expenses knowing that they can negotiate a good deal at an upcoming major show.

The downside of this approach is your existing customers. I have seen existing customers come onto the stand and buy up big on the show special. This looks good on the sales chart initially, but it is usually followed by a slump while they use up their bargain purchase. The total volume of sales is usually only slightly increased—if at all—but the margin is down.

The real value of a show special is that it attracts *new* customers who may become long-term clients. In that sense, it may even be worthwhile as a loss-leader. The only way to know where the balance falls is to track the results.

## Handbills

You may want to try handing out handbills at the show. Target them. They should offer a benefit to your target market. If they offer everyone a chance for a trip to Hawaii, you are *not* filtering out your clients.

Target them further by dressing your aisle-walkers in a billboard with a qualifying question on it: *Do you want to save money on your printing costs?* or *Do you want to reduce adhesive drying time by 23 hours? Ask for our leaflet here.* Keep it simple, so it can be taken in at a glance, and let prospective clients qualify themselves.

Train your people to ask a qualifying question. Instead of, 'Hi! Would you like a brochure?' have them say, 'Hi! Are you a printer?' If you have people wandering further afield from the aisles around your stand, be sure to include a map of how to get to your stand on your handbill, and some reference points, such as the organiser's office and the café, so that the visitors can orient themselves.

I also recommend that you test how well this works. Hand handbills out on one day and not on the next, and see if there is a significant difference in traffic to your stand.

It goes without saying that you should check with the organiser before you launch your people into the show with handbills.

## Post-show activity

While you are planning your show, it is absolutely vital that you allow resources for the post-show follow-up. You have spent a lot of money and effort to get those show leads and, if you do not follow up, you are wasting a lot of business.

You have to allow for temporary staff, for the cost of doing a post-show mail-out, perhaps for software that will allow you to do it more easily.

Following-up is covered in more detail in Chapters 12 and 13.

Should you use *a telemarketing service* as part of your post-show activity? That depends on the number of leads you have and how you have generated them. Your staff should be able to cope with the leads they have personally collected.

However, you may want to consider using a telemarketing service when you have generated a large number of leads through such methods as competitions or the organiser's list of visitors.

A competition list can be a high-quality reservoir of your potential clients when you have a prize that only they would find attractive. The organiser's list will be most valuable if you can search it effectively so as to separate out your target market.

Telemarketing can achieve a variety of ends. For some products, it will generate direct sales. For others, it can be used to make appointments or draw up a short list to be contacted by your own salespeople.

Choose your telemarketer carefully. Some are better than others, and they do not come cheap. Monitor the results to see if the return justifies the expense. If you do decide to use a telemarketing service, you need to budget for it now, while you are planning the show.

# Dressing for the show

There are only two ways you should dress at an exhibition: as you normally dress for business, or in a uniform.

## Dressing for business

If you are not going to dress in a uniform, then dress for business, the way you normally do when visiting your clients (although, seeing how some reps dress, you may have to do better than that).

Sometimes show visitors dress down. For instance, if a show is in an exotic location, such as the tropics or a foreign country, out-of-town visitors in particular may dress appropriately, especially if there is a conference attached to the show. Do not be tempted to follow suit; you still dress for business.

When you meet with a serious buyer, you are in a business meeting. If you normally dress for business in a suit, then dress in a suit.

## Uniforms

Seriously consider putting all your team in matching uniforms. This makes them easier to identify and easier to approach. It also says, 'I am here to serve you' and it makes you look like a team, which is reassuring to visitors.

I have invariably found that a uniform has a good effect on personnel. Because they look like a team, they *feel* like a team. Most of us have a sense of the special feeling of putting on a uniform, even if it is only from school sport. You put on your uniform and you put on a different mind-set—more empowered, more focused, more goal-oriented.

Make sure that the uniform is of good quality and that everyone feels good wearing it. A good self-image is a key component in self-confidence, and self-confidence is *the* most influential element in superior performance. The most common uniform is a coat or blazer of some kind (or, if a more informal look is desired, a shirt), often with the company name and logo embroidered on it.

Sometimes a company will buy only blazers for the team, and then everyone shows up in an assortment of trousers, shirts and skirts. Go the whole hog and get complete uniforms for everyone, and watch the difference it makes to your troop's *esprit de corps*. Be sure to inform everyone of the shoe colour they need to wear.

If you are concerned about the expense, remember that you can use these uniforms over a number of shows. At the end of the show, ask everyone to hold onto their uniforms and store them in their wardrobe until the next show.

# Go through the exhibitor manual

Go through the exhibitor manual as soon as you get it. Do not just scan it. Put some time aside, work through it in detail, and send off any forms that are required.

Organisers have deadlines as to when they want certain information from you. If you are late, you may incur a late fee, or may not get some services at all.

There is information in the manual that you will need, such as move-in times. Often, for a big show, access times to the loading dock are staggered, and you only have a small window of opportunity in which to unload. If you arrive out of your scheduled time, you may be presented with difficulties.

In addition, you may need to distribute information from the manual to a variety of people, including your stand contractor and your transport company.

# Prepare a written action plan

This subject is really the most important of this chapter but, because it cannot be addressed until the subjects above have been attended to, it has been left until last.

Once you have determined what resources you will need for the show, and what has to be done to achieve your goals, the next step is to work out an action plan, put it in writing, and distribute it. It should include what has to be done, who is going to do it and when it has to be completed.

An action plan is best laid out as a table. Below is the format for a simple one that works well enough.

| TASK TO BE DONE | PERSON RESPONSIBLE | SIGNED FOR AND DATE | RESOURCES NEEDED | DATE FOR DELIVERY | ACTUAL DATE DELIVERED | SIGNED OFF |
|---|---|---|---|---|---|---|
|  |  |  |  |  |  |  |
|  |  |  |  |  |  |  |

Take a form like this into the meeting and fill it in as you work out who is going to do what. After the meeting, tidy it up (because it will be full of corrections), type it and make a copy for each individual. Personally distribute the forms, having each person sign off on their own copy and on your master copy. Then you need to monitor the execution of the jobs.

You need to go to all this trouble because an exhibition is often seen by the people who have been asked to participate in it as a lower priority than their normal work, so they keep putting off the tasks they have been given when faced by the more pressing needs of their normal duties. And people just plain forget. If plans are not carried out in a timely fashion, however, the result is a last-minute rush, generally by the person in charge (meaning you!), involving a lot of stress and resentment.

That is also why it is necessary to put the action plan in writing and have everyone sign off on it. Because, to paraphrase the immortal words of Louis B. Mayer, a verbal action plan is not worth the paper it's written on.

Chapter 4

# Three months before the show

- Meet with the full show team

- Prepare a preliminary roster

- Prepare lists of potential clients for pre-show invitation

- Confirm accommodation and travel arrangements

- Plan pre-show training for staff

- Design and print lead forms

# Meet with the full show team

Now, three months before the show, it is time to meet with the team again. This time include not only the planning team who met at the previous meeting, but everyone who will be working on the show, including the sales and technical people, and support staff. Ask everyone to bring their diaries along.

## Brief the team on aims, targets and strategy

Bring everyone up to date. Brief them on the overall aims of the show, and the specific targets the team is aiming for.

Outline the strategy for achieving those targets, as contained in this book, and each individual's activities and responsibilities within that structure, including inviting visitors before the show, gathering and recording leads during the show, and following up those leads after the show.

Outline the action plan and what progress has been made thus far.

## Brief the team on how the stand will work

If you have a stand design, walk everyone through it, using overhead projections of the floor plan and the designer's impression of the stand. Explain how everything will work and how everyone will function within it.

One of my clients has me attend this planning meeting if it is a big show with several divisions of the company involved. In this way, the questions and practical issues that invariably come up can be resolved immediately, thus allowing the process of planning and exhibiting to progress more smoothly and effectively.

# Prepare a preliminary roster

Since everyone who will be staffing the stand is at the meeting, you can allocate times. Ask those who have not brought their diaries to fetch them. This can save you a lot of work later. It will prevent people coming back to you, after you have drawn up the roster, because they suddenly discover, on looking in their diary, that they have something unmissable already scheduled—necessitating your going through the process of scheduling all over again.

Furthermore, it is helpful to give people a long lead for their rostered times, especially if the show runs over a weekend. In this way family and social commitments can be planned around the show.

Nevertheless, consider this a preliminary roster, as you may well find that things change.

In theory, each staff member should be rostered on for a maximum of half a day at a time, the reason being that performance begins to fall off after the first few hours. Staffing an exhibition stand is hard work. It is physically and emotionally tiring to be on your feet for hours on end, keeping your spirits up, while talking with a long sequence of strangers.

However, the fact is that, unless they are very large, most companies do not have the luxury of being able to roster people half a day on and half a day off, and the usual practice is for everyone to be on for the whole show.

But if you really want to maximise the potential of a show you should be prepared to put in even longer hours. You should be meeting with people at breakfast, lunch and dinner. Such a lot of business gets done this way, especially with out-of-town people, that it is a shame to waste the opportunity. It is only for a few days and the pay-off is worth it. Go out. Work hard. You'll be glad you did as the sales roll in over the following few months.

Remember to schedule in the post-show meeting, that everyone will attend, on the first working day after the show. See Chapter 11, *The day after the show*.

# Prepare lists of potential clients for pre-show invitation

In the previous chapter, *Six months before the show*, we covered the pre-show promotions that you needed to start planning because of their long lead times for sending out press-releases and initiating advertising.

Now we look at the more targeted process of inviting individuals, which happens six weeks before the show. You need to start planning it now, six weeks ahead, in order to have the invitation lists ready.

There are two kinds of individual invitations: personal invitations and mail-outs. Inviting individual prospective customers to your stand before the show is a very effective strategy, and personal invitations work best of all. Always do the personal invitations. The mail-outs are great if you have the resources, but never do them at the expense of the personal invitations.

## Personal invitation lists

The personal invitation lists consist of individual staff members' lists and the company list.

'If you had a choice of anyone to come to the stand and talk to you, who would be the top ten people on your list?' This is the question you pose to your sales team and, in fact, to everyone who will be staffing the stand. Hand out worksheets like the one below to everyone at the meeting, and make a start on compiling personal lists.

| PERSONAL PRE-SHOW CONTACT LIST | | | | |
|---|---|---|---|---|
| CONTACT NAME AND POSITION | COMPANY NAME AND ADDRESS | PHONE NUMBER | DATE AND TIME OF APPOINTMENT | CONFIRMATION LETTER SENT |
| | | | | |
| | | | | |

Work with the people at the meeting to see if you can get everyone to write down ten names, even if they do not have their details to hand.

This is a dream list. Get everyone to stretch. Suggest that it should include very senior decision-makers whom they may not normally think to approach. It could include important potential buyers in an area somewhat outside their normal market, people who are not directly potential clients, but who could be important influencers, individuals they have been trying to get to, or meaning to get to, and those to whom they have spoken previously and would like to speak to again.

You will find that while some prepare a very adventurous and ambitious list, other lists will be most practical, even mundane. This is fine. The purpose of making up these lists and getting in touch with the people on them is two-fold. First, they will generate meetings with important potential clients and may result in significant business. Second, they change your people's thinking, moving them from a passive mind-set to a proactive one, where they are driving what is happening on the stand and lifting their vision of what may be possible.

You may find that the initial response from some of your sales team is not particularly enthusiastic. Persevere. It is remarkable how one real success causes the general interest to pick up and results in a more positive attitude next time.

From a company point of view, you may want to use the show to target a specific market. Perhaps you have a new product, or you want to heavily promote an existing product, or you want to push into a new territory. In this case, you may want to create a separate target list of the buyers you would like to talk to. These people could be followed up on a management level or their names distributed amongst the staff, to add to their own list.

The lists do not have to be completed during this meeting, but they do need to be ready six weeks before the show, when the invitation procedure starts. Inform your people of this fact and schedule a meeting for that time in order to go through the invitation process and begin the campaign.

The process is described in detail in Chapter 5, but it is useful now to go through it in brief with everyone, so that they know what to expect. It consists of the following steps:

1. Ring the people on your list to make an appointment to meet them on the stand.
2. Write the appointment in your diary (and take your diary to the show).
3. Follow up with a letter confirming the appointment.
4. Inform others in your organisation who may be interested in being there.

## Mailing lists

The main distinction between a personal invitation list and a mailing list is that the people on the mailing list are not personally contacted by phone. Nevertheless, the invitations that are sent out still need to be personalised: the letters have to be personally addressed to the individuals you want to reach. Depending on the number of people on your list, you can either type individual letters, or type a general letter and do a mail merge on your word processor.

It is important to ensure that your list is up to date and accurate. Some people get personally offended if you spell their name wrongly, give them the wrong title or address their predecessor in the position. Others simply assume that you are going to be similarly slapdash in your service, and they dismiss you.

Lists may be made up from a variety of sources, including your own database of existing or past clients, previous visitors to your stand, a list of visitors supplied by the organiser after previous shows, or a list merchant's offerings.

Your own database of existing and past clients is potentially the most useful and relevant list, since these are people who know you and have dealt with you in the past. You also know them and their business.

After a show, you may be able to get a list of visitors from the organiser. All exhibition organisers have a database of exhibitors, and some also collect a list of visitors for their own marketing purposes. But visitor lists are not collected for every show. For some shows aimed at the general public, such as large 'home' shows and motor shows, visitor details are not recorded. When the doors are opened, the people simply stream in.

When it comes to trade shows and some smaller and more tightly targeted public exhibitions, such as personal finance shows, the organiser will usually collect visitor details through registration on entry. Besides general contact data, these may include specific interests the visitor has, usually through a series of multiple-choice questions that can be easily put into an electronic database.

Electronic formats are generally the most useful forms of visitor databases. They can often be searched according to various criteria. For instance, the database of a personal finance show might yield people who are interested in retirement, personal investment, home loans, and so on. An electronic database may also be able to be imported into your own customer tracking software.

Find out the format the organiser uses, which database software it is compatible with and the fields by which it can be searched. If it is not compatible with your own software, a purchase may be worth your while, just so you can search the list, or there are companies that will do the conversion.

List merchants sell lists targeted at particular demographics. The quality can vary widely and, if you want to go down this route, ensure that the list is tightly focused on your target demographic and covers the region from which you want to draw your customers. That way you will not be wasting your resources contacting the wrong people. Ask how often the list is cleaned and updated. When was the last time? What proportion of the list was checked?

But in the end the only way to know how useful this kind of list is going to be is to try it and keep a record of the results.

## What is the priority of contacts?

If you have limited resources, I highly recommend that you contact the staff and management personal lists before the others. They are likely to be by far the most effective.

Also ask yourself how many visitors you can handle. Any bottleneck in your processing of potential clients is likely to be due to the number of people on your stand, and generating more traffic may not be particularly valuable if you do not have enough staff on hand to cope with the traffic that is already coming through.

However, if you have the resources, by all means use other ways to generate more traffic to your stand. Better an embarrassment of riches!

# Confirm accommodation and travel arrangements

As was mentioned in Chapter 2, *Twelve months before the show*, some accommodation arrangements need to be made well ahead of time. If shows are in regional centers, quality accommodation may be limited. In extreme cases you may not get any at all if you leave it too late.

But even if your exhibition is in a large centre, quality accommodation close to the venue can go quickly, so it is wise to book your stay well ahead. It is best if the exhibition and your hotel are within an easy stroll of each other. Check with the show organiser, as special rates will sometimes have been arranged for exhibitors at nearby hotels.

Having accommodation close by allows you to have a relaxed breakfast before the show and walk in, rather than have to face the traffic. Similarly, it makes for a far more relaxed end to a tiring day. It can also make it easier to have breakfast or dinner with clients, especially if they are staying in the same venue.

# Plan pre-show training for staff

Training your staff is crucial for a successful show. It is the most important element of your strategy and can literally make the difference between success and failure.

There are two areas of training that will give your staff the skills they need in order to function at their best:

- Training in your own and in your competitors' products
- Training in visitor management skills.

Training time needs to be scheduled into the two weeks preceding the show, in order to ensure maximum recall, but it needs to be planned now.

# Product training

One of the common complaints of show visitors is that the people staffing stands don't know their own products.

Your people are the embodiment of your company, and visitors will judge it by the experience they have with them. If your people appear incompetent, the visitor will tend to assume that your company is incompetent and will be reluctant to do business with you.

Staff need to present your product in the best light if they are to persuade potential customers to buy it. Even the most experienced staff can benefit from a refresher course. If you have non-salespeople on the stand or if you are showing new products they are unfamiliar with, there is an even greater need for them to become thoroughly acquainted with what you are offering.

In addition, some visitors attend shows to do some comparison shopping before they make a final decision on a purchase, so it is important that your stand staff have at least a general understanding of your main competitors' products.

Your prospective clients will be talking not only to you, but to your competitors as well. They will be asking direct and indirect questions about how your product compares with the competition. Your staff need to be able to highlight the benefits of owning your product, and also how these benefits make your product more attractive than that of your competitor.

Find out which of your competitors will be exhibiting at the show and concentrate on those.

## Product demonstrations

Demonstrating a product is one of the key elements in filtering your clients out of the passing crowd and onto your stand. When you do a demonstration (preferably on the aisle) it tends to stop those who have an interest in your product. Those who don't have an interest keep on walking, which is desirable, as you do not want to talk to them in any case, since this wastes valuable time you could be using to talk to real prospects.

The purpose of a demonstration at an exhibition is not to explain your product so thoroughly that the observers feel they have enough information to make a decision to purchase or not. It is to emphasise the benefits to be gained from your product, so that onlookers will be interested to find out more. At this point the next level of filtering, namely the stand staff, can take over.

A good demonstration is, therefore, a specialised skill, and needs to be learnt and rehearsed before the show if it is to be effective. Some of your people may be good at this kind of thing, but are *all* of them?

Who is going to be doing the demonstrations? Only specified individuals or everyone? If some of your people have not done these demonstrations before, or if new equipment is involved, rehearsing them ahead of time will allow you to notice where people may need guidance to improve their performance, and where you need to provide additional resources. This may save you the embarrassment of public failure on the stand, which will not only be uncomfortable, but may result in lost business.

Thus, to recap, at this meeting you may need to decide who is going to be carrying out demonstrations, who will need training, and who will handle the training. It is recommended that you schedule this training during the same session as the product training discussed above. That way even those who may not be doing the demonstration themselves, but who will be using it to approach visitors, can become familiar with it.

Another reason to plan now is that the demonstrators and the trainer may need the intervening time to get equipment and materials ready and prepare the scripts.

Product demonstrations are discussed in more detail in Chapter 7.

## Visitor management skills

As we have stressed, your staff are the most important element of your show. They will make or break it. Imagine putting up your stand and having no staff on it for the several days of the show. How many sales would an empty stand make?

To be at their most effective, staff need to be clear as to who they are targeting, how they will interview visitors to determine if they qualify as potential clients, how they will record visitor details and rank them in order of importance, and how to begin and end conversations gracefully. These skills do not come naturally, but through training and rehearsal.

This topic is so important that there is a whole section devoted to it in Chapter 7.

# Design and print lead forms

You need lead forms on the stand because you need to record potential clients' information if you are to follow up effectively. You cannot rely on your memory, no matter how good it is. After all, you may be talking to hundreds of people at the show. And writing on the back of business cards is strictly for amateurs.

The forms printed out by some visitor-tracking systems supplied at shows can be useful as an adjunct to your own lead forms. You can print out and attach the visitor's personal details to your own lead form and so avoid having to write them down. But I recommend that you still have your own custom-designed lead forms.

A custom-designed form allows you to record all the information you need to follow up successfully. But, because of the way it is laid out, it also helps the stand staff structure their interviews with visitors properly, prompting them to ask all the questions they need to ask.

Some companies favour a smaller size form that can be carried around in the coat pocket for a quick draw. They also feel that a smaller form is less intimidating. We experimented early on with such forms, but found that they were too small. A full sheet allows you to record as much information as you need and encourages both your staff and the visitor to keep talking, instead of stopping because there is no more room to write.

The forms are kept at central points on the stand and there is never a problem, when talking to a genuine client, in asking them to step over to a table or counter so that information can be recorded. And far from being intimidated, genuine buyers like to be taken seriously enough that you want to record what they have to say.

Below is a sample form. You can design your own, but I suggest that you incorporate all the elements you find here. More information on the use of the subject lines in the form will be found in Chapter 7.

## EXHIBITION VISITOR RECORD

Exhibition: _____  Date: _____

Name: _____

Position: _____

Company: _____

Address: _____

Phone number: _____

Fax: _____

Email: _____

Areas of interest: _____

1. _____

2. _____

3. _____

4. _____

A B C D

Additional information: _____

_____

_____

_____

Next contact: _____

Contact requirements: _____

Other interested parties: _____

RE: _____

Record taken by: _____  Date: _____

Chapter 5

# Six weeks before the show

- Begin the pre-show invitation campaigns

- Write the follow-up letters

# Begin the pre-show invitation campaigns

In the previous chapter, *Three months before the show*, one of the tasks was to prepare lists of people you would be inviting to your stand. As you already know, the lists can take the form of:

1. The individual salespeople's list
2. A list generated by the company
3. A mailing list.

Now, between four and six weeks before the show, it is time to contact the people on those lists, before they have filled up their exhibition diary.

## The personal invitation campaign

You will have scheduled a meeting for this time with those who have been preparing personal invitation lists. Remind them of the meeting and ask them to bring along their lists. It may be wise to give them some notice, in order to allow those who have been putting it off to finalise them.

The lists should include the people's name and position, company name and address, and telephone number.

The purpose of the meeting is to learn the invitation procedure so as to actually begin the campaigns. The invitation procedure consists of the following steps:

1. Ring the invitees to make an appointment to meet on the stand.
2. Write the appointment in your diary (and take your diary to the show).
3. Follow up with a letter confirming the appointment.
4. Inform others in your organisation who may be interested in being there.

### Rehearsing the invitation

You need to rehearse your invitation. This is a sales call, and you are selling an appointment. As with all sales calls, you will have more success if you have rehearsed what you are going to say. This means writing a script, trying it out on each other and modifying it in the light of feedback, until you get something that works.

There are a number of things you may want to include in the invitation. For example, it is preferable to have a special reason for the meeting, rather than just a general invitation to see your range of products or services. Busy people who go to shows generally have limited time, and an agenda. There are probably a number of companies they specifically want to see, perhaps a particular area in which they want to do some research, and they may leave themselves some free time just to wander around.

Your invitation has to be so interesting that they will make the time to see you. For that reason you need to sell them on the potential benefits you can offer them. So rather than tell them about the special features your new product has, tell them what it could do for them—save them money, increase their production, reduce their down time, and so on.

Pitch your talk at the level of the person you are addressing. If you are talking to a maintenance manager, you need to talk about your product in terms of maintenance; if it is a company accountant, it will be in financial terms. You may need to develop more than one approach to use for different people.

## Sell the appointment

The purpose of your phone call is to make an appointment. It's great if your prospective client starts asking you questions about your product—it means they are interested—but avoid getting into a selling pitch on the phone. The danger is that they will think they have enough information to make a decision whether to see you.

If they want to know more, suggest that because it sounds as if the product is of real interest to them it may be preferable to wait until you get together on the stand. Then you can answer all their questions and also new ones which will probably come to mind when the product is actually there in front of them.

You need to have both your diary and the stand roster with you when you are ringing people. The roster is to ensure that you are going to be there when they are, and the diary will prevent you double-booking. Ask what days they will be at the show and suggest a couple of time-slots when you will make sure you are on the stand. Once they have agreed to an appointment, write it in your diary, thank them and tell them that you will send a letter confirming the details. Tell them that you will also be including a complimentary pass to the show (if you will be) and ask if they would like more than one for others who may be coming with them.

If you are not personally going to be on the stand at the time they want to come, then refer to the roster and tell them the name of the person who will be there. Assure them that you will inform that person to expect your guest. Confirm that arrangement in the letter you send.

As soon as you get off the phone, fill in the details in the form letter that you will have prepared previously and make sure it is typed. It should thank them for the appointment, confirm the time and briefly summarise the benefits they will gain from the meeting. The envelope should include the complimentary passes, if appropriate, and a map showing how to get to your stand. The letter should be sent on the same day that you spoke to the person, if at all possible.

## Complimentary tickets and a map

Some shows are free to visitors while others charge an entry fee. As an exhibitor, you generally get a certain number of complimentary tickets to give out. Depending on the show, the organisers may also give you additional tickets if you ask.

If it is free entry, most organisers will give you as many invitations as you want. After all, it is in their interest to do so, since the more visitors there are, the better. One organiser was somewhat taken aback when one of my clients asked for 1200 entry tickets, but was very pleased to supply them.

Even if you have to pay for the tickets, consider it a good investment to send them to a limited number of the prospective clients you would really like to talk to. Put it in the context of your total show expenditure. And besides, they can hardly neglect to come to your stand if you've paid for them to come into the show, can they? Include a map of how to find you.

## The pay-off

Pre-show invitations may seem like a lot of work but if a dream list was really drawn up, consider the potential business that could flow from it. It is part of the process of establishing a relationship with a future client. If, as it is said, it takes five contacts on average to get a new client, then when you meet the person on the stand, it will be your third communication—the first two being your phone call to make the appointment and your confirming letter with the invitation. By the time you have carried out the post-show follow-up that is outlined in Chapters 11, 12 and 13, you will have sent them two letters, had two telephone conversations and you will be sitting down to your second face-to-face meeting. That is six contacts. You'll be old friends.

Do remember to take your diary to the show—not only to remind you who you are expecting, but also to make future appointments.

## The mail-out campaign

The same rules apply to the mail-out as to the personal invitations. What you are selling is the visit to your stand. Make it sound exciting, make it sound new and, of course, sell benefits rather than features. Include any special deals that you are offering, but don't make it a product brochure.

While you won't be personally following up the letters with a phone call, they still need to be addressed to the recipient personally. You'll get a far better response than with a general flyer. You know how you yourself respond to most flyers . . . As above, include a map of how to find you and complimentary tickets if you can get them for free.

## Email

Email can be a superb medium for contacting your prospective clients. It is quick, you can personalise it through a mail-merge with the right software and you can create a rolling campaign. And, best of all, it is cheap. You can email thousands of people for practically no cost. There are email lists available for rent or purchase from list merchants.

However, we should all know by now to be wary of spamming, the practice of sending mass unsolicited emails, especially of a commercial nature. Spamming is bad net etiquette; it infuriates some people and can bring upon your head severe reprisals. These can include 'flaming', which is abusive email (never answer back), and denial of service by your ISP.

Promotional campaigns via email are a whole subject in themselves. If you want to try it, there are books on the subject, but my recommendation is to start small and expand as you grow in experience and skill.

Start with your existing and past clients and people with whom you are in regular contact and, again, personalise. Do not send out generic email, although you can include an attachment which is the same for everyone. The attachment should contain all the information, including show dates, times, a map, details of your product, special offers. However, this should not be a product brochure. Remember, you are selling a visit to your stand. The attachment should also be printer-friendly.

If you want to get really fancy, you can attach a link to the exhibition website, if it has one and if it is worth looking at.

Your covering email should always be addressed to an individual, along the lines of:

Dear Jane

If you're going to [the exhibition] on [date], I thought you might be interested in seeing the new [offer/product] that we'll be showing. We think it's very exciting! You'll find details in the attachment.

　　Please email back and I'll send you free entry passes. How many would you like?

Kind regards
John

# Write the follow-up letters

There are two sets of follow-up letters you need to write now and store in your computer for later use. One is the letter confirming the appointment, as discussed above. The other consists of the follow-up letters that are going to be sent to the A-list and B-list leads you will gather during the show. There is more information on these letters in Chapters 11 and 12.

# Chapter 6

# One month before the show

- Finalise the stand roster and circulate it
- Confirm all arrangements
- Hire temporary staff

# Finalise the staff roster and circulate it

By now you should have a final roster worked out. Type it up and circulate it to everyone involved.

# Confirm all arrangements

## Exhibitor manual

Go through the exhibitor manual once more to make sure you have all the timing in hand, and that you have sent off the appropriate forms. The list of these may be extensive and could include additional power and lighting requirements, plant and furniture hire, stand cleaning services, fork lift hire, phone and fax lines and so on.

It is likely that the organisers will have contacted you if you have failed to send in crucial forms. They may not, however, which may mean you will not get certain services at all, so it is best to double-check.

## Stand details

If you are getting a custom stand built, confirm the details of the move-in times with the stand builder. This includes both the time when he can move in to start construction and the time when you can go in to put your equipment on the stand.

The rule here is: the sooner, the better. The stand contractor should get in at the first available moment. All sorts of things can hold up progress during a build-up, and it pays to leave as much time in hand as possible. You should absolutely aim to be set up on the day before the show opens and not be still dressing your stand on the morning of the show. Know how long it will take you to set up your equipment and let the stand contractor know. Agree to a handover time, and confirm it in writing.

Check on the progress of your stand construction. Unless it is very big or complicated, construction may not have started yet, but it does pay to touch base and check that things are on track. Communicate the move-in details to your own staff. Let them know when they'll need to be on site to set up.

## Transportation and storage

Check that you have made all the transportation arrangements for your equipment for both before and after the show. Check also that you have arranged for storage of your boxes and other material not needed on the stand during the show. Sometimes there is limited storage at the show itself, but other times you will have to arrange off-site storage. If you are exhibiting in your home city, it may be convenient to store everything back at your premises.

The official show carter may have facilities to help you, or else your transport company may be able to take things back to their depot and deliver them to your stand again at the end of the show.

## Equipment and supplies

Check that all the arrangements for the equipment and supplies you will need for the show are on track. This naturally includes the product and display materials, but may also include consumables used during demonstrations and samples you will be giving away. If you will be handing out brochures, check to see if you have enough or if you need to print more.

# Hire temporary staff

If necessary, hire temporary staff for the post-show entering of leads into your database, the printing of the follow-up letters and the fulfilment of post-show follow-up material.

You may also be hiring temporary stand staff for such things as handing out brochures and doing your product demonstrations at the show itself.

Chapter 7

# Two weeks before the show

- ■ **Reconfirm all move-in details**
- ■ **Check that all resources and supplies are in hand**
- ■ **Check on your stand**
- ■ **Training**
- ■ **A few considerations to make things easier**

# Reconfirm all move-in details

It is time to reconfirm all the move-in details with the show organiser, the stand contractor, your own staff and the transport people.

# Check that all resources and supplies are in hand

All the resources you will need for the show, such as literature, product and equipment, should be in hand now, ready for transportation to the stand.

As a general rule for exhibitions, it is sensible to have things in hand well ahead of time. This gives you a safety margin for delays, which happen despite the best-laid plans. Exhibitions are a hard deadline, they won't wait and they're quickly over, and too much money is at stake to miss the boat for lack of planning.

# Check on your stand

Check again with the stand contractor as to the progress of your stand.

If it is a contractor you have worked with before and who has proven to be reliable, then it may only require a phone call. However, if it is a new stand or a new contractor, you may want to visit the workshop to satisfy yourself that the work is progressing on schedule.

Chances are the stand will not yet be completed and to the untrained eye it may look as if there is an alarmingly long way to go. This is not necessarily a cause for concern. Most busy professional shops work quickly and plan their work so that it is completed as required.

Sometimes, if a new stand is particularly complex, it will be put up in its entirety in the workshop to see that it all fits together, but often it is only on the show floor that you will see it fully erected for the first time.

Check that the handover will still take place as planned.

# Training

Training sessions in product knowledge and visitor management skills should be carried out in the two weeks leading up to the show, preferably as close as possible in order to maximise retention.

# Product training

Your staff need to know what they're talking about. It bears stating again that one of the biggest complaints of show visitors is that the staff do not know their products. If you have new staff on the stand, or existing staff who are not familiar with your product range, or if you have people from different divisions on the stand, a session to familiarise them with the full range of products is vital.

If there are technical aspects of your products that need to be addressed with show visitors you may need to have technical experts on the stand. Stand staff are likely to be asked detailed questions, and if they can't answer those questions they need to refer the enquiry to someone who can.

Detailed product knowledge is important. Don't try to fake it. If it is a casual enquiry, it may not matter much, but serious potential buyers who know their business will see through you immediately. And there are few things more likely to destroy your credibility than to be perceived as incompetent or untrustworthy. If you try to fake it, that is how you will come across, and people will not do business with those they do not trust.

Even experienced staff can benefit from a product review.

## Rehearse

Your staff will perform much better if they rehearse how they will present your products and services. They need to be confident in what they are doing. First impressions are important. People will go away from your stand with emotions as well as facts, and if they feel uncertainty or hesitation coming from your staff, that is how they will feel about your product.

## The competition's products

Your training session should include a comparison with your competitors' products.

An exhibition is a buyer's market. Your competitors are likely to be there. Some visitors who are there specifically to buy your kind of product or service are walking between stands to do some comparative shopping prior to making a decision.

This is one of the great attractions of shows to visitors. A range of products are available, and it is very convenient to compare them so as to make an informed decision before buying.

Some visitors will ask you direct comparison questions. You need to be aware not only of the features of your own products, but how they compare with features of competing products. More importantly, you need to know how your features provide superior benefits.

Your competitors will be comparing their own products and services with yours and may be putting their product in a flattering light while denigrating yours with varying degrees of subtlety—perhaps even mis-representing you. You need to be able to counter that and present your own point of view impressively.

While you may be able to do direct comparisons between your product and others, you can also do it indirectly. 'Our printer produces twelve pages a minute at full resolution. This is a big speed advantage over other machines that only produce that kind of throughput in draft mode. With this machine you get your print jobs fast! And that means you're not standing around waiting.'

This kind of statement, which also pre-empts the competition if your visitor has not yet been to see them, will not roll smoothly off the tongue by itself. You need to develop these kinds of statements before the training session and then train your people to use them. They need to rehearse. Training and drilling are the keys to good performance.

## Visitor focus rather than product focus

As part of your product training, you also need to remind your people to listen. A common complaint of show visitors is that the stand people are so focused on promoting their product that they do not seem to be at all interested in finding out what the visitor actually wants. This can be infuri-ating and, because they are speaking off the point, quite enough to turn a visitor off a purchase.

Teach your people to listen, ask questions, and listen to the answers. They need to focus on the clients, to find out what is important to them. This is especially important at a show, because time is short, and you often do not have the luxury of the longer discussions you can have in a prospective client's office.

How to interview visitors to determine what they want is covered in greater detail below, in the section on handling show visitors.

## Product demonstration

When you are next at a show, walk around and notice where show visitors are gathered. Almost invariably, it is where there is an activity of some sort going on. Sometimes they involve visitors testing their skills in a fun way, perhaps throwing balls, hitting golf balls or driving remote-controlled cars. Sometimes they are purely entertainment, such as provided by singers or magicians. Or they may be celebrities such as sportspeople.

Even an interesting video can draw people. Sporting videos are among the most attractive, especially ones showing spectacular crashes and spills. I have even seen a stand running a live broadcast of a football game, and it was attracting a lot of people.

All of these can be fun to watch, and they can certainly get a large number of people around the stand. They have the drawback, however, that they are non-selective. They attract everyone, or at least a broad cross-section of the passing crowd.

But the strategy we are employing in this system for exhibiting is, as you remember, to filter out of the passing crowd only those people who are interested in your product or service.

Use the demonstration as a prospecting technique. If, instead of a general-interest demonstration, you *demonstrate your product*, it will tend to attract those who have an interest in it. Those who are not interested will move on, which is exactly what you want. In addition, your staff can move amongst the people watching the demonstration and further qualify them to identify prospective clients.

## Script, rehearse and practise your demonstration

A demonstration needs to be scripted and rehearsed before the show. Its purpose is to engage your target market, show enough to illustrate your main benefits and then invite further discussion. It needs to leave your target audience wanting more.

If a demonstration is to do this effectively, it must be carefully thought out, scripted and rehearsed, and tried out amongst yourselves in order to get some feedback. This is true whether you have your own people doing it or a professional presenter.

Everyone who will be doing a demonstration needs to practise it before the show until they are thoroughly familiar with it.

## But our product/service can't be demonstrated

Some companies say that their service cannot be demonstrated, and they can give all sorts of reasons why.

Find a way. Sit down with your team and brainstorm a way to do it. There is always some method of demonstrating your service, even if it is only a person talking to a video that shows your product in use.

Incidentally, a video on its own, be it a corporate video or one of your product in action, will not do the job. You know this yourself from all the lonely videos you have seen at shows, busily talking to nobody at all. The key is that there is a live person on your stand talking to passers-by and engaging them in an exchange of information.

## Qualify the watchers

Just stopping people in the aisle with a demonstration is not enough, because the normal result is that when a demonstration is over, people walk away, and the stand staff wait, hoping someone will stick around.

Some do, but many who might have stopped, won't. At an exhibition some feel out of their comfort zone. Many people do not enjoy talking to strangers, and if they can find an excuse not to approach you—such as that it is too crowded just after the demonstration and that they will come back later, they will.

So, while one staff member is doing the demonstration, others need to be moving amongst the visitors and asking them if they use, or could use, your service in their own business. This must happen during the demonstration, and not after it has finished.

You can ask simple questions such as, 'Do you use [product] in your own business?' If they do, you can move into a qualifying conversation, and perhaps invite them onto your stand to discuss their business in more detail.

If they say no, move on to the next person. Have a variety of questions ready so that you are not asking each person the same one. You can use the questions you will be asking in the normal qualifying process, as discussed in the next section on managing visitors.

Choose your targets carefully. Prospect with your eyes first. Look for people who are already asking questions. Body language will often indicate interest. Notice the person who is focused and intent or moving in a way that indicates interest, such as nodding or making comments to an associate.

## Length of the demonstration

Keep the demonstrations short and hold them often, remembering that your purpose is to engage buyers and potential buyers to the extent that they want to find out more.

You are wasting a great deal of potential if you have your demonstrations only once an hour. Your prospective buyers are walking past continually, not in hourly clumps. You may not want to demonstrate during busy periods when everyone is talking to visitors anyway, but you can do one whenever you want to talk to more people.

Similarly, you are wasting potential if you have long 20-minute demonstrations that go into exhaustive detail. Either people will get all the information they think they need, or they will get bored. In both cases, they will move on. How long your own demonstration will be will depend on what you are demonstrating, but take five minutes as a guide.

It is good to get questions during the demonstration, as it engages not only the questioner, but also the other people watching. However, be careful not to get diverted from your purpose. Answer briefly if you can, or else postpone your reply:

'Sir, these are excellent questions. I appreciate your asking them, and I want to answer them. However, as you can appreciate, I have a limited time to complete this demonstration. If you can wait until I am finished, I will be very happy to talk to you. Or perhaps one of my colleagues could help you straight away.'

At which point, one of your colleagues does.

## Demonstrate the benefits

It has often been argued that every product is in reality a service. People buy a product for what that product can do for them, for the benefit it provides. When they buy a refrigerator, they buy a product that delivers the service of keeping food cold. This, in turn, produces the benefits of greater choice, less spoilage, fewer trips to the shops, etc. When they buy a computer, they buy a product that delivers a range of services, including perhaps word processing, spreadsheet analysis, email communication, perhaps a games platform, all of which provide benefits.

Benefits are always personal. When people buy a car they don't just buy a product that delivers the basic service of personal transport; otherwise, everyone would buy basic, reliable, safe cars that are cheap to run. The reality is that cars deliver a range of other benefits. These may include personal feelings of excitement and pleasure, pride of ownership, and proof of (and satisfaction in) achievement. They may also provide the service of sending messages to others about the owner, about their wealth, taste, and social position.

So, when you are demonstrating your product, focus not on its technical aspects, but on the services it provides to your clients and, through the services, the benefits they will receive. People, in the end, will only be interested in your product if it benefits them.

## End the demonstration with an invitation

'Ladies and gentlemen, that concludes our short demonstration. I am sure you have lots of questions about how [our product] can [improve your productivity/save you money/etc] specifically as it applies in your own business. We understand that each business is unique. Please come onto the stand and tell us about your particular situation. We would be happy to talk to you.'

Or: 'That concludes our demonstration, ladies and gentlemen. Thank you for your attention. Those of you who have further questions and want to know more about [your product] will find myself and my colleagues very willing to help. Please come onto the stand now. We'd like to talk to you.'

Or make an offer: 'For those of you who have a further interest in our product, we have a special introductory offer that I am sure you will find very exciting. Please come onto the stand now. My colleagues and I would very much like to talk to you.'

These little speeches, like your whole demonstration, should be memorised and rehearsed until they come smoothly off the tongue.

## Should you hire a professional presenter?

This depends on how many staff you have available and on how your own people are able to handle the presentation. It is preferable to use your own people, as long as they are articulate and confident. Even if they are not slickly professional (or perhaps because of it), a company's own people can lend credibility and authority to the demonstration.

You may also be surprised at how much your staff's competence will be enhanced by scripting and then rehearsing the demonstration. If you have run demonstrations previously, you will have noticed how much better they tend to be at the end of a show than at the beginning. Why not cut out the beginnings—via rehearsals?

If you have limited staff, however, then leaving them free to deal with stand visitors by hiring a presenter may be a more effective use of resources.

A hired presenter will need a script and rehearsal time, as well as feedback from you. A presenter is essentially an actor and, in fact, may be one professionally. Be sure to include adequate time for scripting and rehearsals in your agreement. You can determine this in discussions beforehand.

Do not allow either the presenter or your own staff to get 'on stage' unless you are happy with their performance.

## Public address systems

Consider getting a public address system for your demonstrations. It will prevent your voice from becoming strained and ragged and make you feel better and more relaxed. Additionally, it is more effective if you can talk in a normal voice, as it makes individual listeners feel as if you are talking to them personally, rather than shouting at the crowd.

A PA system should augment your voice, not replace it. Get some of your colleagues to stand where your visitors will normally stand and give you feedback. This should be done in the normal show environment, as it always gets noisier once the crowds have come in.

Ideally the people watching should not be aware of the PA at all, only of your voice. Turn the system down to the point where you can speak in a normal voice, but can still be heard clearly. If more than one person will be using the PA, remember your settings.

## Demonstrate with enthusiasm!

Finally, your demonstration should be exciting and enthusiastic! The demonstrators should sound as if they *love* the product! After all, if you aren't excited about your product, why should anyone else be?

# Visitor management skills

In the two weeks leading up to the show, and preferably as close as possible to it, it is vital to train everyone in the basic skills of managing show visitors. How potential clients are treated by your staff, before, during and after the show, is the measure of your success at that show. That is the cutting edge at which relationships are formed.

An exhibition is a special environment where sellers and potential buyers meet briefly and decide whether they want to meet again. If an exhibitor relies on the visitor to get in touch, they will have far fewer sales than if they follow them up themselves. Staff need to interview visitors to determine if they are potential clients, record their details, and follow them up after the show.

These are not natural skills. If they were, every person on every stand at every show would be doing it right. But in fact very few do.

These skills need to be learned and practised in order to be mastered. Just *telling* your staff to do it will not get you good results.

What follows is the material that is covered in the training workshop *Staffing an exhibition stand*. It is generally delivered as a half-day workshop on our clients' premises. Since its inception in 1990, the workshop has been under a constant process of evolution and improvement, in the light of practical experiences in real exhibition situations. Many hundreds of companies, ranging from small family concerns to major transnational corporations, have trained thousands of staff through these workshops, with excellent results.

It is recommended that everyone who will be working on the show attend. This includes not only the staff who will be on the stand on a day-to-day basis, but also management and support staff. These people are important to the whole process, and it makes for greater productivity and goodwill if they know how their activities contribute to the overall project. People are more cooperative and motivated if they feel they 'own' the project.

In the course of the workshop the participants learn what is, for most of them, a new approach to exhibiting and rehearse the six basic skills for managing exhibition visitors that are described below. This training has a twofold purpose, or rather two complementary aspects of the same purpose.

The first is to outline a new strategic approach to exhibiting, and change the participants' approach from essentially passive to proactive. By the end of the workshop, they will have moved from seeing themselves as waiting on the stand for visitors to arrive and then describing the company's product and answering any questions about it, to a position where they are driving the operation and actively looking for clients.

The second purpose is to learn the six basic skills for managing exhibition visitors, which form the practical application of this new strategy.

## Putting the staff's role in context

As was outlined in Chapter 1, the strategic approach of the system described in this book is to use the exhibition as a process of progressively filtering clients out of the general population. For the purpose of workshop training that process is elaborated here.

There are four levels of filtering: the organiser, the stand, the people who are staffing the stand, and the post-show follow-up.

### The first level of filtering is the organiser

An exhibition happens within a certain 'catchment area'. This may be local, regional, national or international, depending on the show. It represents a general population of thousands, perhaps many millions, of people. Clearly not every single one of these people is a potential client.

The organiser promotes the show through a variety of means and so filters through the doors a certain number of people who have an interest in the exhibition and thus, potentially, in what your company offers. As a result, we have in the exhibition hall a greater concentration of potential clients than there are in the general population. Indeed, this is the main reason that exhibitors pay to attend such an event.

Again, however, not everyone walking around the aisles is a potential client. The proportion of show visitors who are potential clients will vary from show to show and exhibitor to exhibitor but, in any case, it is only a percentage of the people walking past the stand.

How do we filter them out of that stream and onto our stand?

### The second level of filtering is the exhibition stand

The primary purpose of an exhibition stand is to filter *onto it* those people who are prospective clients, and to filter *off it* those who are not.

The most important thing you can do to attract potential clients is to demonstrate your product, as that draws those who have an interest in it, and does not attract those who do not, so they keep walking. This and a number of other things that can be done to make a stand more attractive to the right people are covered in more detail in Chapter 3.

### The third level of filtering is the people who are staffing your stand

Even with the best-designed stand, not everyone who comes onto it is a potential client. That is where the people who are staffing the stand come in—they are the third level of filtering, and the most important one. Their main task is to interview visitors in order to determine if they qualify as potential clients and, if they do, to record their details so that they can be followed up after the show.

For this to happen effectively, the people who are staffing the stand need to know three things:

1. exactly who it is that they are targeting at this particular show
2. the questions to ask that will determine if the person they are talking to qualifies as a member of this target group
3. how to record the visitor details on special lead forms.

The skills that are covered in this workshop will allow them to do all that effectively.

### The fourth level of filtering is the post-show follow-up

Most companies do not have a systematic process for either collecting or following up the leads they get at an exhibition. They are missing out on a lot of business. How much business? How does a 30% increase in market share sound? That is the increase that one of my clients, a major multinational corporation, achieved in a particular market segment after they implemented the system described in this book. This was the result of changing their approach *at one show* of an exhibition they had been attending for years.

What has been outlined above is the strategy for getting new clients. What follows in the rest of this training session is the practical implementation of that strategy, in other words, the tactics.

## Six skills for managing exhibition visitors

Obviously the role of exhibit staff is to manage show visitors. They will be at their most effective in carrying out this task if they have the skills that enable them to do it.

Six skills have proved to be the core competencies transforming performance:

Before the show
1. Inviting potential clients to your stand

During the show
2. Identifying four categories of visitors
3. Interviewing and qualifying visitors

4. Recording and ranking visitors' details for follow-up
5. Starting and ending conversations

After the show
6. Following up the leads in ranked order.

## 1. Inviting potential clients to the stand

The procedures for inviting people to the stand before the show have already been covered in detail. You may already have prepared the lists and made your invitations. In that case the workshop is a good opportunity to discuss how the process worked and learn from each other's experiences.

If the pre-show invitation process has not yet been implemented, there may still be time for each person to draw up a short list and make some invitations, depending on how long before the show this workshop is being run. Information on how to go about it is covered in Chapters 4 and 5.

## 2. Identifying four categories of visitor

It has proved useful to put visitors into four categories:

A  Buyer
B  Potential buyer / Influencer
C  Non-buyer
D  Tourist

At a show there is only a limited time to talk to people. If it is a popular show, it is literally impossible to get to every potential client, there are just too many. Moreover, potential clients need to be identified quickly so that exhibition staff do not waste time talking to the wrong person. Otherwise, an exhibitor could spend a half hour explaining his services and products to someone who is not a buyer, while ten people who *are* potential buyers come onto his stand and leave again because they are not being served.

Staff need a system to ensure they are talking to the right people so as not to waste opportunities. Before the show, they need to identify very clearly exactly whom they are after—not only their target market in general, but much more precisely, exactly the kind of person who represents this category, right down to job description and duties.

## Who is a Buyer?

Buyers are decision-makers. They have the authority to buy from you. They are in the market for your product or service.

The buyer is the prime person you are looking for at an exhibition, the one most likely to become your client. He or she may fall into one or more of the following categories:

- They are there specifically to buy *your* product or service. (Lucky you!)
- They are actively looking for the particular product or service that you provide, though not necessarily yours. They may be at the show doing some comparison shopping amongst suppliers before they make a final decision.
- They are facing a problem in their business and are looking for solutions. Your product provides a solution.
- They are changing some aspect of their business (for example, setting up, upgrading, replacing, wanting to change suppliers) and are researching how to best go about it.

## Who is a Potential Buyer?

Like buyers, potential buyers are decision-makers and have the authority to buy from you. In addition, potential buyers now use, or could use, the kind of product or service you offer, and you may be able to convert them into buyers, now or in the future.

They may not already be your client for one or more of the following reasons:

- They are using your competitor's product. (You may be able to persuade them of the advantages of switching to yours.)
- They may not be in the market right now. (When will they be?)
- They may not be aware of your product, or aware of the advantages of using it. (You may be able to persuade them of those advantages.)
- They may not know that they need your product, or that your product can fix a problem they have. (That is, until you point out the upside of using your product and the downside of not using it.)
- They may have a misapprehension about your product. (You can set them straight.)
- They may be changing some aspect of their business. (Your product or service could be just the thing to help them do it.)

## Who is an Influencer?

Influencers can be put into the potential buyer category because, in practical terms, you treat them the same way.

Influencers are people who are not themselves buyers, but who influence the buying decision. They could be at the exhibition in either a formal or an informal role.

Formal influencers may be at the show specifically to gather information. They may be there alone or as part of a team, and will be reporting back to a buyer.

A company may send a team to a show to gather information if it is planning to make a major purchasing decision. For this reason a team could be very important to an exhibitor. Members might come onto a stand together, in which case the team may be comparatively easy to identify, or they could be operating separately and planning to get together later to pool their information before making a final decision or short-listing suppliers.

Teams can come from both the government and industry sectors.

Keep alert for formal influencers. They may only be lowly end-users of your product and, as such, not the ones not who decide whether to buy it or not, but they might have been brought to the show specifically because of their hands-on experience. You can only know a person's true status and purpose by questioning them.

Other formal influencers can include consultants, specifiers, engineers, maintenance people, safety officers, and so on. You can make your own list as it applies to your particular industry and service.

There is also a variety of informal ways in which people can be in a position to influence decisions others make. It could be that they constitute a so-called *centre of influence*, meaning that they are influential figures, conduits for information, in an informal network. Often they are respected in their particular field or senior persons in their industry. These people are sought out for their advice and, since they often like to give it, keep themselves informed.

An informal influencer could be someone who knows a potential buyer for your product and will talk to them about it. A person like this could be a very good source of a referred lead.

Some influencers may identify themselves as such but, as with most stand visitors, you will probably only be able to identify them by means of careful questioning.

## Who is a Non-buyer?

Non-buyers do not use your product or service. They may be decision-makers, but they have no use for your product. They are not buyers, nor potential buyers. They are not influencers.

Such a person may show strong interest in your product, may even ask lots of very intelligent questions, but may simply be gathering information out of a general curiosity. One of the main reasons people go to exhibitions is to keep abreast of the industry, to see what is new in the field and to educate themselves both by attending seminars and talking to people at the show.

Non-buyers could also be visitors killing time before they have to go back to the office, or while they are waiting for their friend to finish visiting another stand.

You need to identify these people early and, if it is a busy time on your stand, politely move on from them.

## Who is a Tourist?

This person is wasting your time. He or she is someone from the next stand who is bored and wants someone to talk to, or is the competition, or is a retired industry person there to catch up with old colleagues. In a public show the tourist could well be a relative of someone on the stand.

Identify these people fast and move on to interview someone else. Remember that your mission is to find new clients, and your time is limited. What about students? They are often looked upon as a nuisance. In fact, one of my clients equates students with locusts because, he says, they descend on his stand like a swarm and strip it bare. Brochures, samples, giveaways, food, displayed products—anything that is not nailed down—may disappear. When he sees students coming, he does a pre-emptive strip of his brochures and giveaways.

Yet, students are the buyers and influencers of the future, and it might be sensible to treat them well. If you are particularly busy, explain your situation and invite them to look around the stand while you attend to business.

## What do you do with existing clients?

Your existing clients are your most important asset. It is five times more expensive to get a new client than to keep an existing one. However, a show is at its most useful and profitable when it is used to gain *new* clients. Unless you are up-selling or cross-selling (that is, trying to upgrade their purchasing patterns or to sell them something new), consider carefully how much time you want to spend with your existing clients.

This is not to say that you should rush them off the stand, but it may be more time-effective to see them out of show hours—at breakfast, lunch, dinner and during breaks—rather than have long talks with them when they show up, especially if it is busy.

When they do come to the stand, suggest lunch or dinner or, better still, if you know beforehand that they are going to the show, make an arrangement to meet them off the stand.

## 3. Interviewing and qualifying visitors

The first job of exhibit staff is to qualify visitors. This may involve a change of mind-set. Staff generally go onto a stand ready to talk about their product or service, sometimes very enthusiastically. They want to tell everyone about how good their product is! This is great, of course, but first they need to be sure they are talking to the right person.

The show strategy, as we know, is to filter clients out of the passing crowd of strangers. Because of limited time at the show, it is not possible to talk to everyone. There will be many potential clients who will not become clients because of lack of time to speak with them. Additionally, not everyone who comes onto the stand will be a potential client, as we saw in the previous section. Therefore, exhibit staff need to talk to as many people as possible and to sift through them quickly until they come to a representative of their target market.

Thus, when a stranger walks onto the stand, the staff need to take a proactive approach to the meeting. Quickly but courteously, they must interview and classify the visitor as a buyer, potential buyer, influencer, non-buyer or tourist.

They want to know quickly if this person is a buyer or potential buyer so that they can then move on to either making a sale or recording information to use for following them up after the show.

The process is as follows:

1. Interview the visitor to determine if they are a client or potential client. Do not move on to product demonstration or discussion until you have determined this.
2. If they are a non-buyer or a tourist, thank them for their time and move on.

3. If they are a buyer or potential buyer, show and discuss your product features, while further qualifying their specific needs.
4. Ask if they are making a buying decision at the show. If the answer is 'yes', move into a sale. If the answer is 'no', take the lead by writing down their details for post-show follow-up.

A stand visitor is interviewed by asking questions designed to qualify them as a buyer. They may be questions about the person's role and position, about their company if they work for one, what it does, how many people it employs, and so on, depending on the criteria that have been determined before the show. These questions will make it clear if this is the right *kind* of person to be talking to.

Further questions may be specifically about the person's interests and needs, and more precisely still, the reason they have come to the show.

The following are examples of the kind of general questions that can be asked. Each exhibitor, in addition, will have more specific questions relating to their own business. These are best brainstormed during the training session.

*What does your company do?*
*How big is your company? How many people do you employ?*
*Are other company members here as well?*

*What is your position in the firm? What are your specific duties?*

*Which equipment do you currently use?*
*Who is your supplier?*
*How do you deal with [some common problem that your product solves]?*
*What are you wanting to achieve with . . .?*
*Do you make the decisions about [your product]?*
*Are there others in your company I should be talking to?*

*Are you looking for something specific at the show?*
*What is your central reason for being at the show?*

*What's the timetable for this?*
*When will you be making a decision about it?*
*What is your budget?*

## Questioning technique

Visitors to your stand will not always answer your questions openly and freely, of course. They may be reticent for a number of reasons. They may even be under the impression that they are interviewing you!

When a visitor asks you a question, always answer it, but do so briefly and return to your own interview plan. If you can springboard off their question, all the better. The classic, of course is: Customer: *'Does it come in red?'* Salesperson: *'Would you like it in red?'*

In practice, the conversation may be a little like a table tennis game, with questions and answers being batted back and forth. The important thing to keep in mind is that you are interviewing them to determine if they are a potential client for you.

## Keeping customer-focused

It is important to keep customer-focused rather than product-focused at a show. In the excitement of a show, exhibitor staff can get so caught up in their product, and so interested in showing it off and explaining it, that they completely miss the point, which is to service their customers' needs. It is good to keep in mind that a potential buyer is not really interested in your product as such, but in the benefits it can provide to them. As far as they are concerned, the subject under discussion is themselves and their needs and if those are not addressed, they can get annoyed and leave.

It is important, therefore, to be initially customer-focused. Only after you have determined what their needs and interests are do you turn to your product. At that point, you can far more effectively talk about it, because you are actually still talking about their needs. Your product features become solutions to their problem.

And once you've solved their problem, the rest of the sale may only be a matter of mopping up the details.

## When to sell and when to get a lead

Salespeople are by training and instinct inclined to close every prospective customer. This can be very wasteful behaviour at an exhibition. Most companies make the bulk of their sales not *at* the exhibition, but *after* it. A strategy of gathering leads, combined with a systematic follow-up, is usually the best approach. Indeed, it usually results in a dramatic increase in business.

However, some people do buy at the show, and one of the most important

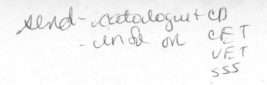

questions to ask someone, after it has been established that they are a buyer or potential buyer, is: 'Can I ask you at this point whether you intend to make a decision to purchase at the show today? Whether you're open to that possibility? Or do you intend to gather information and make a decision afterwards?' If the answer is 'at the show', then by all means go ahead and make the sale, if you can.

Selling at a show is no different from selling anywhere else. The same process has to be gone through: establishing a need or desire, explaining and convincing the customer that your product will fix the problem or satisfy the desire, and closing the sale. Yet, many companies have made up their minds that they cannot get sales at a show, and so they do not even try. Ask for the sale. You may be surprised!

If, however, the answer is 'I'll make the decision whether to buy after the show', you should either make a specific appointment to see the visitor later (and write it in the diary that you've brought to the show), or get their details so that they can be followed up.

## 4. Recording visitors' details

Unless you record visitors' details you cannot follow them up. It is as simple as that.

Most companies make the bulk of their sales, if not all of them, after a show. And yet, as noted previously, these very companies do not have a systematic procedure for following up show visitors. Sometimes there is an attempt made, but too often, no action is taken at all.

One of the main reasons for this is that details of prospective buyers are not recorded. A company may come out of a show with a collection of business cards but, without information to go with them, it is difficult to know which to call and what to say. Some leads do get followed up, of course. Sales people put hot leads into their pockets and get in touch after the show.

This is very ineffective use of the resources of a show, and very wasteful of the opportunity that it presents. Even with the best intentions, relying on a pile of business cards and memory is inefficient when one is talking with hundreds of people over several days. Visitors who could have become customers get lost.

If there are to be effective follow-ups, ones that will lead to successful sales, the people on the stand need to gather *detailed*, *written* leads. And for this they need custom-designed lead forms.

*Teacher – Private studio – performer*
*university*
*students – junior int senior*
*program' how long teaching*
*Doing ET now? using? members MTNA*

## EXHIBITION VISITOR RECORD

Exhibition: _____ Date: _____

Name: _____
Position: _____
Company: _____
Address: _____
Phone number: _____
Fax: _____
Email: _____

Areas of interest: _____
1. _____
2. _____
3. _____
4. _____
A B C D

Additional information: _____
_____
_____
_____

Next contact: *Followup* _____
Contact requirements: _____
Other interested parties: _____
RE: _____

Record taken by: _____ Date: _____

Above is an example of a lead form. Each company will need to design its own, so as to suit its own business needs, but it is recommended that the elements in this example be retained unless they simply do not apply.

## Explanation of the headings

*Exhibition*
The details of the show at which this lead was taken go here, and the date.

*Name and contact details*
If the visitor has a business card, attach it here. This section of your form should be large enough to accommodate a card. Attaching a card, rather than writing the details, saves time and reduces mistakes. Alternatively, if a visitor tracking system is being used, the printout can be attached to the form. Staplers are the easiest and quickest to use, and the most secure. Ensure that there are staplers on the stand.

*Areas of interest*
In this section, you may want to specify your product lines or services. This allows you to sort the leads after the show, as appropriate.

*A B C D*
This is your ranking system. A: *Buyer*, B: *Potential Buyer / Influencer*, C: *Non-buyer*, D: *Tourist*. If you circle one of these at the show, you can quickly sort your leads afterwards and follow them up in order of importance.

The 80/20 rule applies to the leads many companies collect: 80% of the business they get from the show comes from the A leads, which generally make up about 20% of the total. You will, however, probably find that as your staff become more adept, the proportion of A leads will increase.

*Additional information*
Here write any additional information that comes up in the conversation.

This may include more specific facts about the person's needs, company details, personal information, others who may be involved in the decision-making process—in fact, anything that may help whoever will be doing the follow-up. Generally speaking, the more detail the better.

When you think you've got everything, a very useful question is: 'Is there anything else I should know?'

*Next contact*
When have you arranged to contact this person again? In most cases, that will be straight after the show, but sometimes the visitor will have a specific time in mind, depending on budgets, projects, or business plan timetables.

This point could be very important. If they ask you to contact them in six months' time and you ring immediately after the show or, on the other hand, if they tell you they want to make a decision within the next week and you ring them in three, you will not only look unprofessional, but you may miss the sale altogether.

*Other interested parties*
This sounds better than *referrals*. Remember always to ask anyone you talk to for referrals, especially influencers. Referred leads are very important. It is much easier to make a sale to a person to whom you have been referred by someone they know than to sell cold. And yet it seems to be one of the most difficult things for salespeople to remember to do, which is why a prompt is included here.

When requesting a referral, use an open-ended question and phrase it in the plural. In other words, do not ask, 'Do you know anyone who...?' because the easy way to reply is 'no' and, in any case, you've only asked for one person. Ask: 'What other people do you know who might find our service/product helpful? I'm thinking in terms of...' and here you list your target market. This automatically starts the visitor thinking in a more focused way and about multiple people.

When you have asked for a lead, poise your pen over your paper ready to write, and wait. It takes time for people to think. Don't interrupt.

*RE:*
This section is for the subject heading of the follow-up letter you'll be sending the visitor immediately after the show. For example:

Dear Jane
RE: IMPLEMENTING A NEW ACCOUNTING SYSTEM IN YOUR
BUSINESS
    It was a pleasure to meet you at the Money Show on Thursday...

*Record taken by*
This is for the name of the person taking the lead.

Generally leads are collected in one or more secure places on the stand. This usually takes the form of a box or bench-top with a slot into which everyone puts their leads. These are regularly collected for safekeeping and, subsequently, taken back to the office for processing.

In general, it works best if the individuals who took the leads follow them up, in which case their names on the forms allow them to be appropriately distributed. However, there are some other reasons why it may be useful:

1. If someone else is going to follow up, they may need to get in touch to clarify some point.
2. You may want to keep track of how individual staff members are performing.
3. You are using a reward system to encourage quality and volume of lead collection.
4. The person who will be entering the information into a database will need to include this information.

### Legibility and thoroughness in lead forms

A lead is useless if it is illegible. There can be a tendency to rush during the busy periods of a show, but staff need to take the time to fill out the form legibly; otherwise, all their work can be wasted. If people have illegible handwriting, they should print.

Additionally, lead forms need to be filled out thoroughly. Personal shorthand and cryptic notes won't do. The person completing the form should think that they are writing for someone else to read and understand. This may literally be true; they may not be the person following up a lead they take. So this is truly a case where you should do unto others as you would have them do unto you!

But even if stand staff are writing for their own use they cannot rely on memory. Over the period of the show they may be talking to hundreds of people. Some they will remember, but others will blur into each other and the details will escape. Thorough notes will still allow effective follow-up.

## Visitor tracking systems

Some shows give exhibitors the option of using a visitor tracking system. Often this entails having a 'smart card' reader on the stand: the exhibitor swipes a visitor's identification card through the reader that either produces a printout or records their information electronically, or both.

At their simplest, these give the exhibitor no more information than is on a business card. Some go further and can be programmed with a series of categories that can be checked off as they apply to individual visitors. They may also provide a small space on the printout to write in further details.

All this is not enough, however, and a custom-designed form works better because:

1. The exhibitor may need to record more information than can fit on the printout.
2. Having a detailed form to fill out prompts staff to ask questions of the visitor that they might otherwise forget to ask. In the busy environment of a show it is easy to forget important details, so a custom form acts as a reminder.
3. Visitors will sometimes think of other information that the exhibitor should know as they watch them fill out the form.

However, an electronic tracking system does give some benefits. In the first place, some people do not have a business card with them, and it is quicker and more reliable to print out their details and attach them to a lead form than to write them by hand.

Secondly, some tracking systems also record visitor details electronically. Contact details in an electronic format may be more easily transferred to an exhibitor's own electronic database.

Perhaps more importantly, using the tracking system supplied by the show organiser may give the exhibitor access to a larger database of visitors. If this database can be searched electronically via appropriate categories or fields, it may provide a very high quality resource for post-show follow-up. It can enable the exhibitor to get in touch with potential clients they missed at the show.

Nevertheless, a tracking system should not replace an exhibitor's own custom lead form, but should act as an adjunct to it.

## 5. Starting and ending conversations

Many people find it difficult to start and end conversations at a show. Generally, it is not the middle of the conversation that presents the difficulty, since they are talking about a subject they are familiar with, namely their product and the client's business. It's the hello and the goodbye.

This may well be a natural human trait. Research suggests that we all have an initial wariness towards strangers, especially if we are alone. It's hard-wired into us. It may be a comforting thought that the person approaching you is feeling just as much out of his or her comfort zone as you are.

Having said that, a great deal of this discomfort may stem from simple uncertainty about what to do, and individuals find it much easier if they have a few opening approaches and a few closing strategies at the ready. In other words, what they need are a few scripts. A script, just like a film script or a play script, is a series of instructions on what to do and what to say; you learn it and rehearse until you are doing it well. Below are a few suggestions.

### *Initiating conversations—Script 1*

Someone comes onto your stand. You smile, step up to them, look them in the face, shake hands and say: 'Good morning/good afternoon, I'm [your name] from [your company].' Then you look at their badge, look back into their face, and say:

'[Their name], what can I do for you today?'

or:

'[Their name], what brings you onto our stand? Are you looking for something specific?'

Then you listen to what they have to say and move into the qualifying questions we covered earlier.

Remember that *you* are interviewing *them*. You are asking them questions about themselves and their company. Does this person qualify as a buyer or potential buyer of our services? Your purpose is to start them talking about themselves.

## Initiating conversations—Script 2, the elevator speech

An elevator speech is how you might answer the question 'What do you do?' if it were asked of you in an elevator. You only have the time between floors to reply. The elevator speech is in a question-and-answer format that presents a problem in the form of a question and then the solution in the answer. It goes like this:

*there's never enough time n ETFSSƎna*

'You know how [an activity or a problem which is faced by your clients]? *lesson*

Well, we [provide the solution *and* the benefit].'

*have [    ] study tools for spain students that lets them work at home a before n after lessons inspain studies*

Examples might be:

'You know how annoying it is when the bathroom mirror fogs up? Well, we manufacture bathroom mirrors that don't fog, which makes using them much more pleasant.'

'You know how you have to keep replacing the cutting edges on your drag buckets? Well, we manufacture a cutting edge that wears 20% more slowly, so reducing your costs.'

This script can be used after you have introduced yourself, or if a stand visitor asks a general question about your company, or its products and services. For example, after a visitor has come onto your stand and you have introduced yourself, you might go straight into: '[Name], can I tell you what we do here? You know how . . .'

## Initiating conversations with people in the aisle

Some people will stop in the aisle and look at your stand from there. The aisle is neutral territory, they are safe there. Not if you can help it!

Walk to the edge of your stand and ask any of the qualifying questions that were covered earlier. Better still, do what one of my clients does—he walks out into the aisle, turns and stands beside them looking into stand with them and then does a variation of his elevator speech: 'I bet you're looking for a way of reducing your finishing costs.'

Some visitors laugh and get into a conversation, but some just walk away. Does the stand staffer expect to engage everyone? No. He's increasing his odds.

## Ending conversations

It seems difficult sometimes to end a conversation. Perhaps the visitor just won't stop talking and you can't find an opening in which to end it gracefully. Some people are afraid to offend by seeming abrupt.

*When* to end a conversation is comparatively straightforward. If it is a non-buyer or tourist, the time to move on is as soon as you have identified them. If it is a potential buyer, you end the conversation after you have recorded their details on the lead form. As soon as that is done, you need to move on.

Certainly one should always be courteous to a visitor, but it needs to be borne in mind that a show is a series of business meetings and that time is limited. Exhibitors do not have enough time to talk to everyone that they need to, so when a conversation is over, they must turn to the next person.

*How* to end a conversation sometimes presents more difficulty. It helps enormously if you have a few simple strategies. Again, you need a script.

With a non-buyer or tourist, you're welcome to use my closing script. With appropriate variations. It runs:

'[Name], it's been a pleasure talking to you. I'm sorry, but it looks like we can't help you today. Thanks for stopping by on the stand. I hope you find what you're looking for somewhere else at the show. Good luck!'

While I'm saying this, I give them a big smile, shake their hand, and turn and walk away.

How do I interrupt the person who won't stop talking? I just nod at whatever they happen to be saying and jump straight in. It gets easier with practice. I notice as I watch my clients that they develop the use of all sorts of body language to signal they are about to end the discussion, express their regrets and soften the message.

Another way to get rid of someone is to use the lead form or the visitor tracker. Just say: '[Name], this is very interesting. Would you mind coming over here? We need to get some details.' Take their card, staple it to your lead form, smile, shake their hand and say, 'Thanks, [name], that's great. Thanks for stopping by on the stand. I hope you enjoy the rest of the show.'

If all else fails, you may have to set up an emergency signal. Once I trained some stand staffers for an insurance company. They were all young women who had been hired as customer representatives for their pleasant manner and had been further trained to be nice to people. Their biggest difficulty, they told me, was how to end conversations. Since they were going into public shows where the visitors were from the general population rather than business people, they found they had a high proportion who saw it as a day out and just wanted to keep on chatting.

We arranged for an emergency signal. When one of the girls saw another patting the top of her head as if rearranging her hair, she was to come over, apologise for interrupting, and inform her that she had a phone call. This allowed the first girl to excuse herself and leave.

The girls had a lot of fun rehearsing that one, and it worked very well at the show.

Ending conversations with potential buyers is generally easier. When you have completed the lead form, it is quite straightforward to say something along the lines of: 'This is great, [name]. I'm glad you stopped by the stand. We'll get some further information to you in the mail over the next three or four days, and we'll be in touch soon after. Enjoy the rest of the show. We'll talk soon.' Shake hands and escort them off the stand. 'Bye!'

In the case of potential buyers and influencers to whom you do not necessarily want to talk immediately after the show, after you have competed the lead form you could say: 'Thanks, [name]. It's been a pleasure to talk to you. We'll get some information to you in the next week or so. If there is any other way I can help you, please get in touch.'

The above scripts are just suggestions. You may need to write a number of your own and try them out on each other until you get a few that work for you.

It is important to rehearse your scripts. They need to be learnt and rehearsed until they roll easily off the tongue. You need to be confident in your delivery if you going to use them with strangers in the stressful situation of a show.

There's a temptation to change your scripts during the run of the show. Sometimes this is for the better, and you make worthwhile improvements. But take care that you don't change them simply because you've become bored with them.

We can imagine that because we're bored with them, the show visitors must be bored as well. Remember that they are hearing them for the first time. As long as your delivery isn't boring, they won't find them boring.

You spent a lot of effort developing scripts that work. They are a good tool. Keep using them.

### Being businesslike

It is all right to be businesslike on a stand and get to the point. You do not have to make witty remarks, you do not have to be funny. If you can remember to smile, that's great.

However, serious buyers are there to do business, and all that is necessary is for you to be interested in them and listen properly to what they have to say. If you have a solution to their problems, you have a perfect fit.

### How to keep unattended visitors on the stand longer

There are times when everyone on the stand is busy talking to people while other visitors are standing around, clearly wanting to talk to someone. These busy periods can happen at any time.

Stand visitors will not wait around long. If you yourself have stood around waiting to be attended to, you know that you quickly become impatient and move on. There are a lot more stands to see, and a lot more people selling the same product. People may say to themselves that they will come back later when it is less busy, but they often don't.

An exhibitor can extend the time that people will wait for them by the simple expedient of acknowledging them. This can consist of as little as a nod and a smile, or turning to them and saying something like: 'Good morning. I'll be with you in a minute. Perhaps you'd like to look at [some aspect of your stand] while you're waiting.'

It is important when doing this to excuse yourself to the people with whom you are speaking. This technique can also serve the purpose of signalling to the people with whom you are currently talking that the meeting is winding up. When you turn back to them, you may find that they start doing the wind-up themselves.

### 6. Following up the leads in ranked order

The final skill set that needs to be covered in this training session on how to manage visitors, is how to follow up after the show. This is covered in detail in Chapters 11, 12 and 13.

## Getting help with staff training

Training your staff in the skills described here and in the rest of the book is vital if you are to make a big improvement in your show results. As has been said before, it can make the difference between success and failure.

If you have the skills and the time, you can use the information contained in this book to create your own workshop for your staff. Alternatively, you can get the *Staffing an Exhibition Stand Workshop Kit*, which offers the workshop on tape, forms and worksheets for the participants, and facilitator's notes that will help you guide your staff through the process.

This is the same workshop that I have delivered to hundreds of companies. It is like having me in your training room (only at a very small fraction of the cost!).

You can find more information on www.showright.com.

# A few considerations to make things easier

## The value of teamwork

With some companies there may be a diversity of interests on the stand. For instance, there may be people from different divisions there, who are selling different product, or people who handle different territories. There can be a temptation in this kind of situation for each person to look after their own interests, or at least to be indifferent to the interests of the other team members.

So the person who handles Territory A meets a show visitor who happens to be from Territory B and, thinking that this person is of no use, bids her or him a pleasant goodbye. This is a mistake. It is much more beneficial to everyone if the exhibit staff all work together as a team, helping each other.

The logic is very simple. Which would you rather have—you yourself working on the stand alone, or with every other person on the stand qualifying visitors for you and introducing them to you? The answer is obvious. So, if you find yourself talking to someone who is not a potential client for you, but *is* for someone else on the stand, you inform them of that fact, then take them over and personally introduce them to the appropriate person. It is important to make this personal introduction rather than just point the person out.

If the person the visitor should be talking to is not on the stand or is busy with someone else, and the visitor can't wait, then take the lead, carefully writing down the details, just as you would if you were doing it for yourself.

The end result is that *everyone* on the stand gets more good leads.

# Practical advice on maintaining energy levels and keeping up performance

The reason for recommending four-hour shifts for stand staff is that performance naturally tends to drop off after a couple of hours. Staffing a stand is hard work. It is physically tiring to stand on hard concrete all day, it is mentally tiring to concentrate and talk to many people in a short space of time, and it is emotionally tiring to maintain a good attitude, even in the face of difficult people.

While most exhibit staff do not have the luxury of being rostered on for only four hours at a time, there are a number of things they can do to help maintain their energy levels.

## Drink lots of water

Keep up your water intake. This is one of the most valuable pieces of advice you can receive. It is easy to get dehydrated at an exhibition, and when you do, your effectiveness can plummet by 50% and more. Dehydration can sneak up on you without your noticing. By the time you are thirsty, it is too late. You are already dehydrated.

You need to drink more than you normally do. You are losing water through perspiration because you are physically exerting yourself more than usual, and you are losing water through respiration since you are doing more talking than you normally do.

It should be still water. Not soft drinks, and not coffee.

I recommend that you keep bottles of water to hand in your cupboard or storage area or, better still, consider hiring a water cooler. You can get one from a show supplier recommended in the exhibitor manual or from a supplier in the phone book.

Drink regular small quantities throughout the day. Depending on your body weight, you should be drinking about 2 litres a day.

## Eat well

It is often difficult at an exhibition to eat well. The food facilities that are usually found in a show hall are not renowned for their cuisine. But do try to avoid living on fast foods, and on coffee and cakes. If you can't get anything but fast food at lunchtime and during your breaks, at least make up for it by having a healthy breakfast and dinner.

## Limit your alcohol intake

The opportunities to drink at a show are many. There are cocktail parties and dinners, perhaps also lunches and dinners with clients, and there is the evening get-together with your fellow workers.

Alcohol is a depressant and it hardly needs saying that if you overdo it, it can severely impair your performance on the stand. Certainly you should not drink during show hours, such as on your lunch break. For a start, visitors will smell the alcohol on your breath and this can offend some people. Even those who do themselves drink can be turned off by alcohol on the breath in the middle of the day.

Even if you disguise your breath with mouth fresheners, your performance will be impaired. It will also be impaired when the effects of the drink wear off, and you are left dehydrated and low in energy—perhaps with a headache as well.

If you cannot go without a drink, drink moderately.

## Don't party too hard

Let's be blunt. You are at the exhibition to work, not to party. Of course you should spend your evenings with clients and potential clients. This is a great way of doing business at exhibitions. However, that does not mean that you cannot get to bed for a good night's sleep.

If you are hung over and tired from insufficient sleep, you are not doing justice either to your company or to yourself.

## Get the weight off your feet

Standing on your feet all day on hard concrete is hard on your body. Your feet, knees and lower back, in particular, are vulnerable to pain. You can help to alleviate this by taking the weight off those joints at intervals. Though, as a general rule, I do not recommend seating on a stand, a few high stools placed around it can provide wonderful relief.

Use them just to prop on when there is a break in the visitors. It takes the pressure off the joints and allows them to lubricate again. The advantage of a stool is that you are not really sitting *down*, and you can smoothly come to your feet if a visitor walks onto your stand.

Periodically through the day, you can also take the weight off your joints and lubricate them by standing on one leg and rotating the knee and ankle joints of the other.

Finally, standing on a concrete floor all day is hard on your feet. Make sure you are wearing your most comfortable shoes that are compatible with how you are dressed.

## Take regular breaks

Unless it's very busy, take a five-minute break every hour and a fifteen-minute break every two hours. When you take a break, even a short one, by all means sit in the café (or better still, in the comfortable chairs of the exhibitors' lounge, if your show has one).

However, try to get outside for a brisk walk of five minutes. This will provide you with a short aerobic exercise, which will flush your system with fresh air and get all your juices flowing, and it will lubricate your joints. It will also give you a change of scenery and allow you to come back to your stand refreshed.

Each of the above actions is small in itself, but they can add up to an enormous difference in how you feel and how you perform through the show. If you follow this advice, you'll find yourself at the end of the show with a lot more energy and enthusiasm, and probably with a lot more to show for your efforts.

# Keeping it in perspective

It can get dispiriting at a show to keep approaching people and getting rejected.

If you, as the show manager, have done research on what proportion of show visitors are potential clients for you, then it may be useful to let your staff know. If they know that only one in ten is a potential client, it can change their attitude. They will then *expect* that nine out of ten people will say no, so they can be more cheerful about it.

In fact, you can suggest that they can say to themselves 'Excellent! They said no! Everything is working to plan! Only (nine, eight, seven, six, five, four, three, two or one) more to go before the next customer!'

Of course, if your stand is working well at attracting visitors, then the proportion of potential buyers will be greater than the show average. But don't tell your people this. Let them think they are on a winning streak. They'll be more cheerful.

# Chapter 8

# The show build-up

- The show build-up
- Start your build-up at the first available moment
- Personally monitor the progress of your stand construction
- Meet the organiser
- Check on your competitors
- Expect the unexpected

# The show build-up

The building of your stand and the display of your product are important, and you need to supervise them carefully. There are few things more stressful, and guaranteed to set you off to a bad start, than to still be frantically dressing your stand as the show opens and the first visitors start walking up the aisle.

Your aim is to have your stand completed on the day before the show opens. The construction should be finished and all your equipment displayed to your satisfaction in time enough that you can go back home or to the hotel and have a relaxed dinner and a good night's sleep. That way you can come back in the morning refreshed and ready to face your visitors.

In order to help you achieve this you should start your build-up at the first available moment and personally check on the progress of the installation.

# Start your build-up at the first available moment

Ensure that you start your build-up at the first available moment. It almost always takes longer than you think to put up your stand, and things routinely do *not* go according to plan. You need to allow as much time for dealing with the unexpected as you can.

Check in the exhibitor manual, or with the organiser, to find out when is the earliest that you can come in to start your construction. It may not be at the nominal start time. Sometimes times are staggered so as to prevent congestion, though the organiser will tell you when this is the case.

When build-up times are short, and the dock or loading facilities are limited, you may be given a specific time during the day when you can have access to the dock. Come in on time. If you arrive outside your scheduled time, you may experience difficulties and delays.

# Personally monitor the progress of your stand construction

Nearly every show is, to some extent, a first-time event. Construction crews do the best they can, but instructions and plans can be ambiguous and incomplete. If you have not been there to monitor progress, you have only yourself to blame if you arrive at your completed stand and find that aspects of it are not as you envisaged it.

If you have organised services yourself, you need to be on site to coordinate deliveries and ensure that they happen. Via phone or in person with the suppliers on site, confirm all the deliveries of product, materials, furniture, lighting, phone and fax lines, A/V equipment, etc., and ask for approximate delivery times. Remember to include your own colleagues if they will be helping you install equipment or product.

Expect delays, but if something does not happen when it was supposed to, check it immediately, as build-up time is short and often one thing depends on another. Contact the supplier, either on the phone or in person if they are on site.

Take with you a file with all your suppliers' contact details and the written agreements between you. Also bring along a credit card or chequebook. Paperwork can disappear, or you may find you need something unexpectedly, and you may need to arrange for its supply on the spot.

Try to stay on your stand and check deliveries carefully against your list. Sometimes the wrong thing is delivered, and it is often easier and quicker to fix matters then and there, while you have the company representative with you.

## If you are using a stand contractor

If you are having a custom stand built, or are having a contractor install an existing stand, the contractor will probably try to start installation as soon as he can. However, you need to check. He may have more than one stand in the show, or he may planning to start your stand later, for a variety of reasons.

Let him know when you need to move in. Work out how long it is going to take you to set up your equipment and displays, and tell him. Get his agreement and confirm it in writing.

However, be aware that the contractor may be under time pressures himself, sometimes from the organiser. Build-up times seem to have been progressively shrinking in recent years as organisers try to contain or reduce costs by cutting down on the hire of the hall. Your contractor may also be delayed while waiting on subcontractors such as electricians and riggers. Remember, too, that beyond a certain point, you cannot hurry the construction of a stand.

There is usually no point in going to check on the progress of your stand for at least the first half-day of construction, as it is taken up with unloading, sorting out material, and basic construction tasks such as laying down the carpet. Generally it's useful to go in some time after lunch, but check with your builder.

If it is a new stand, go in with your plans and drawings early in the construction process and carefully check every aspect. It is not unknown for a stand to be built facing the wrong way, or even on the wrong space. It can be helpful to discuss your job with the site foreman, especially if this is the first time the stand has gone up.

Check with the contractor as to when he wants *you* on site. He may need your advice on such issues as the placement of display and graphic elements, and to know where you plan to position your equipment, so that lights can be pointed in the right direction. He will also want you to do a final check before he hands over the stand and sends his staff off.

Make sure you are on time. It is just as stressful for the builder to have his people standing around clocking up costs as it is for you to be waiting for him.

## Letting a contractor do it all

If you normally arrange some services yourself, consider letting your stand contractor do it all. Under this arrangement, the contractor is responsible for everything on the stand, including arranging ancillary services like power, lighting, furniture, signage, plants, A/V and computer equipment, and so on. You simply walk on with your product, set it out, do the show, then pack up and walk off at the end.

It is true that you will pay more for this service, but it might be less than you imagine. The mark-up that the contractor puts on outside services is largely offset by the trade discount he gets. Get a quote. It might be worth it in saved time and reduced stress.

# Meet the organiser

When you get to the show, go over to the organiser's desk and introduce yourself to the desk staff and the show manager. The organiser's staff are there to help you. You will almost invariably find them courteous and helpful. If, during the show, you have an issue that needs to be sorted out, you will find you get a better reception coming along as a friendly face they know.

Things do go wrong at shows. This is normal. A show is a first-time event in which hundreds of people, crowded together, are trying to construct something they may never have constructed before in a short space of time.

However, experienced show organisers have sorted out your particular kind of problem many times before. It is rare for a problem not to be fixed before the show starts. Nonetheless, expect to have delays and expect to wait after you've been promised something. This, too, is normal.

## Check on your competitors

While you are supervising your display, have a look at what your competitors are doing. You may learn something useful from their stand. If you are on chatting terms, say hello.

Knowing what your competitors plan for the show may be helpful when you are briefing your stand staff.

## Expect the unexpected

Finally, expect that in the controlled chaos of an exhibition build-up, unexpected things will happen. The most common problem is running behind schedule. If you do find yourself in this situation, bear in mind that some things can go on simultaneously. If you can get access to some parts of the stand to work, other finishing tasks—such as adjusting lighting and stand cleaning, even some construction work—can carry on around you.

When something does go wrong, keep your cool and stay solution-focused, not problem-focused. Calm and clear communication of the problem, followed by a description of what you need, will generally result in a solution being found. Antagonising people will only slow things down, but a good crew, if they are on your side, can draw on their experience to make things work. Despite everything, stands usually get finished on time.

# Chapter 9

# During the show

- The role of the stand manager

- Managing visitors

- Coaching staff

- Maintaining an up-to-date schedule

- Keeping an eye on the competition

- Learning from the show itself

# The role of the stand manager

There are five main areas that have to be managed during the show:

1. Visitors
2. Staff
3. The stand
4. Competitors
5. Learning from other exhibitors and the show itself.

It does not have to be the same person who does all this, as different duties can be delegated to different people. Some areas, such as managing visitors, will be carried out by everyone.

However, it is the role of the stand manager to ensure they all happen.

# Managing visitors

As we have emphasised, your primary purpose at the show is to sell your product and to gather qualified leads that you will follow up after the show. If your company is like most, your most important activity is gathering leads.

Everything that follows in this chapter is designed to help you and your staff achieve that objective to your maximum capacity.

# Coaching staff

Especially through the first morning of the show, and throughout the first part of a new person's shift, monitor individual staff members' performance and coach them.

## Encouraging the use of their new skills

Check that they are using the new skills they learned in training: that they are interviewing visitors to determine if they are potential clients; that they are customer-focused rather than product-focused; that they complete lead forms with all relevant information recorded legibly.

Often you will find that individuals do not start using their new skills at all. Many people find an exhibition a stressful experience and, under stress, people revert to older, more comfortable routines. Encourage them by pointing out that any new skill feels awkward at first, but gets better and more natural with practice.

It takes time for new skills to bed down. Do not assume that because staff have been trained, they will therefore be doing everything right. Though we roleplay and rehearse the new skills in the training session in order to give everyone practice in using them, like all skills, they need to be practiced over and over.

Keep a multi-show perspective and do not expect perfection. Your people will improve from show to show, especially as they complete a full cycle of activity and see the benefits.

Encouragement should be offered on evidence of improvement, not for 'getting it right': 'That's great! Your lead forms are much more legible now. Thank you.'

## The first morning

On the first morning, before the show starts, call your team together for a pre-show briefing. Re-focus them on what you are there to do and how you are going to do it. Summarise your objectives for the show and the strategy for attaining them. Run over the material covered in the training sessions, including:

1. Precisely whom you are targeting
2. The need to gather qualified leads by interviewing people to find out if they are potential clients
3. The importance of completing the lead forms thoroughly and legibly
3. What the competition is doing.

## Daily briefings

At the end of each day, get together with your team briefly and discuss the day. What were the visitors like? How many leads did you get? What was the quality? Was anything learned that can be applied on the following day?

Congratulate everyone on what they have achieved.

In the mornings, let staff know what progress is being made in reaching your targets, and review the coming day's targets.

## Briefing new staff

Throughout the show, brief new staff members on an ongoing basis as they come on at their rostered time. Do a briefing similar to the one you did for everyone on the first morning of the show, and also give them any other information that may be relevant. They may need training on the lead tracking equipment, for instance.

Do not leave anything to chance, or assume that it will be done by someone on the stand. If you can't be there to do it, designate someone.

## Ensure that people are taking breaks

Except during very busy periods, make sure that everyone is taking regular breaks—five minutes at the end of each hour and 15 minutes at the end of each second hour. People will be much fresher and perform much better if they do so.

## Water, water everywhere

Encourage people to maintain their water intake. Lead by example. Though you can't make them drink, you can at least lead them to the water cooler to have a drink yourself and offer a cup when it's time to have a chat. Keep in mind that when your people get dehydrated their effectiveness plummets, and that will impact on your show results.

## When checking and collecting leads

Check the leads at intervals and when you empty the leads box. Ask the staff for clarification of anything obscure, or ask them to improve their writing if something is illegible. This is good feedback for them. They may think they're doing all right.

If you have time, it may be useful to discuss the A leads with those who took them, as they may remember more information than they actually wrote down. This is also good feedback for them on how to interview future visitors better and complete lead forms.

# Maintaining an up-to-date schedule

Ensure that there is an up-to-date schedule on the stand where everyone can consult it. Thus, if a visitor shows up wanting to see a particular person who is not there, they can be informed as to when to come back.

# Keeping an eye on the competition

By now your stand staff should have a pretty good handle on the competition. You will have covered their products as part of the product training session you held in the last two weeks. You will also have had a look at their stand during the build-up and before the show. Brief your staff on any new developments and any new strategy for dealing with them.

Some companies even send spies to opposition stands in order to find out what they can. They also send all their own staff past the stands so that they can see the people and be on their guard should competitors come onto their own stand.

However, all this can be over-emphasised. You should know a great deal about your competition anyway. If they want to, they can easily send someone you do not know to your stand to pretend to be a buyer. And if you or they are running a show special, you are not exactly trying to hide it—you are splashing it all over your stand.

The best way of dealing with your competition is to stay focused on your customers. Show them how your product or service will help them and give them immaculate service, and you will not really have to worry too much about the competition. Remember the old saying: a good sales team with an inferior product will always outsell a bad sales team with a superior product. Train yourself to be a good sales team.

# Learning from the show itself

During quiet times you and your staff will find it useful to go out and learn from others at the show.

## Assess stand staffing

Evaluate the way you deal with visitors in comparison to the way others do it. Observe a stand from a distance and watch the staff in action. Stay long enough to see complete transactions, from the time a visitor approaches to the time they leave. You will learn a surprising amount in that time.

Go onto other people's stands and pretend to be a visitor. Resist the temptation to talk shop, one exhibitor to another, but act like a visitor and ask about their products and services. Observe how they perform and learn from it. Copy what they do that you like, and make sure you are not doing what you don't like.

Do the same with your own staff. Stand outside your stand for a while and watch.

## Assess your stand position

Take your floor plan with you and walk around show. Note where the main traffic flows are through the show and mark them on your floor plan. Pay close attention to where the light is good. Light is very important. People instinctively find brightly-lit places more attractive than gloomy ones. A well-lit stand is much more attractive to people than a dark one (and that is a central design feature of a good stand), but the ambient light in the hall is important, too.

Choose some positions that you think would be better than where you are currently, and mark them. Try to book them for next year.

## Compare your stand

Walk around and compare your stand with others, with a view to making changes for the following show. In particular, look at those stands which are about the size of yours and at those that seem to have spent about your budget. Study both the stands you like and the ones you don't.

Why do you like them? Why don't you like them? Which are attracting a good number of visitors? Make notes. You will find them useful when you plan your next stand.

Chapter 10

# The pull-out

- Someone needs to be there

- Check on the details of the pull-out with the organiser

# Someone needs to be there

Someone from the company needs to supervise the removal, packing and transportation of your product and materials from your stand at the end of the show. Transport must be organised ahead of time. Unless you have specifically arranged it with your stand contractor, you cannot rely on them to do this.

The pull-down of a stand after the show and, to a lesser extent, the build-up, are the most likely times for things to disappear. Goods can get lost, and they can get stolen. With hundreds of people streaming past them at the doors, the security personnel have no way of knowing or, realistically, of checking if all the goods that people are carrying out really belong to them. The industry abounds with horror stories of valuable goods being stolen.

But even apart from theft, unless someone is supervising the pull-out, things can get left behind. It is not unheard-of for an exhibitor to forget a stand altogether. Many times my crews have rung clients to remind them that they still had goods and equipment on the stand. Often we have packed up clients' goods and taken them back to our workshop for safekeeping.

People leave behind computers, A/V equipment, briefcases, product, expensive signs, boxes of brochures, calculators, all kinds of office equipment, and personal belongings.

When an exhibitor has hired a standard exhibition stand (shell scheme) from the organiser, the pull-out crew will pull the stand down and leave everything else lying on the ground. It is common to see people walking around and picking through what has been left behind.

Sometimes the show organisers will put the goods aside and ring an exhibitor to let them know that they are there, but sometimes they won't. At the end, anything that is left in the hall is treated as rubbish and is dumped by the organiser or the exhibition venue staff.

# Check on the details of the pull-out with the organiser

Check the specific move-out times with the organiser or in your exhibitor manual. Often you have a limited time to move out. There may be a noon deadline, for instance, and it will be embarrassing if you show up after lunch.

Also the nature of the pull-out can vary from show to show. Sometimes, at the end of a show, no-one can take anything out and the venue is locked up until the next morning. In this situation you should come in as soon as the doors open the following morning. At other times, only goods that can be carried by hand can be taken away at the end of the last day; the transportation of larger equipment and the dismantling of the stand itself must be left until the following day. It is tempting in this case for people to leave everything there, thinking they will do it all the following morning. Perhaps they are tired, or they want to go out to celebrate. However, someone needs to be responsible for removing valuable portable goods from the stand at once. If your people don't do it, someone else might . . .

At still other times, the whole exhibition has to be packed up and cleared out of the venue on the day that it finishes. You need to know this and to have the people and transport arranged to do it, rather than have it come as an unpleasant surprise.

If there are things you cannot take when you take your goods away, such as signs affixed to walls, specifically ask your stand contractor to take them back to his premises, from where you can arrange to have them picked up, or else wait until your stand is dismantled and take them.

Suspended banners are often taken down by the organisers towards the end of the pull-out period, when there are fewer people in the venue and cranes can manoeuvre around. If you would rather not wait, check with the organiser what is to be done with them. Sometimes organisers keep them to be picked up later, or they may be left at the venue. Perhaps your stand contractor can take them for you. Whatever the case may be, make the arrangements ahead of time, as it can be very frustrating (not to mention fruitless) to be chasing lost banners later.

Finally, you may need more than one person on the stand during the pull-out. If you have valuables that can be easily carried off, then someone should stay on the stand at all times, such as when others are at the loading dock, for instance.

Chapter 11

# The day after the show

- The post-show follow-up

- The next working day after the show

- Organising the leads

- Outline the follow-up procedure

- Setting up a database

- Analysing the show

# The post-show follow-up

A show is not over when it ends, of course. This is when the post-show follow-up begins, and its effectiveness will determine the success of the show.

# The next working day after the show

Before the show, when you handed out the roster for staffing the stand, you would have included in it a meeting for the next working day after the exhibition. Everyone should have that in their diaries, but it is well to remind them at the pre-show briefings and during the show itself.

I suggest you start with a two-hour meeting and assess if that is long enough for you.

This is the agenda for the meeting:

1. Organise the leads
2. Outline the follow-up procedure
3. Set up a database
4. Analyse the show

# Organising the leads

Separate the leads into A, B, C and D piles. The letters, as you know, represent the ranking system for stand visitors that are on the lead forms you completed and collected at the show. 'A' represents buyers, 'B' potential buyers and influencers, 'C' non-buyers and 'D' tourists (or the less charitable names that some exhibitors give them).

## The A list, the buyers

These are the most valuable leads, from where most of your business will come. As was mentioned previously, you are likely to find that the A leads represent 20% of your leads, but provide you with 80% of your business.

You will probably get some business from the Bs, the potential clients, in time, but none from the non-buyers and the tourists.

Sort the A leads into the order in which they will be contacted, the most important ones first. Importance is measured by a combination of size of potential business, time frame for contacting and any additional information in the notes. It may also take note of the subjective feeling of the person who took the lead about the likelihood of business resulting from that contact. Others at the meeting may also add useful information.

The A leads are distributed amongst your sales staff. These are the ones they will personally get in touch with.

If they are not to be followed up by the individuals who gathered them, they need to be labelled with the names of those who *will* be following them up. The person who will be entering them into the database can code them appropriately. This will allow them to be printed out separately for the salespeople and also enable individual results to be tracked by the sales manager.

## The B list, the potential buyers and influencers

How hard you chase potential business through the B list will depend on the circumstances and on your resources. But in the end, the only way you will know its value is by trying different approaches and testing the results.

Many companies send personalised letters to the A list only. Some send them to the A and B lists. Some send personalised letters to the A list and a form letter with a brochure to the B list. And some don't distinguish between the A and B lists and treat them equally.

To some extent, what you do will depend on the show. If it is a small show with a limited number of visitors then it is easy and sensible to send personal letters to everyone. Indeed, in some shows of this nature, every one of the delegates is a potential client (or an existing one). But even with large shows, you may be targeting only a small proportion of the visitors, in which case it may be easy to personally contact everyone of interest.

This may be the case if you are showing a number of different products that appeal to different markets, in which case you can separate them via the 'Areas of Interest' section on the lead form.

Which method will work for you? There is no way of knowing without testing. The question is not whether different techniques will work, because generally any activity will generate *some* response, but whether you have the resources and whether the effort is worth the return.

You might like to try this approach initially: do a mail-out to all the people on the B list, but personally follow up only a sample; then measure the results.

In any case, you would certainly want to put the B list people (which includes influencers) on your mailing list. Remember that these are all potential clients who are not yet in the market for a variety of reasons. Keep in touch.

As for the C and D lists, the non-buyers and tourists, they're clutter. Throw them away.

# Outline the follow-up procedure

At this meeting you also need to outline the follow-up procedure to the sales staff, and establish criteria for performance. This is covered in detail in the next two chapters. It is recommended that you familiarise yourself with them before this meeting.

# Setting up a database

As the sales manager, or manager in charge of the exhibition activity, you will find it very useful to set up a database of the leads, preferably an electronic database, as it gives you greater flexibility and control. You may already have one that you can use, or you may want to write your own, if you have the skills and the time. Otherwise, there are a number of good customer-tracking programs available commercially.

As was mentioned earlier, it could be money well spent to hire temporary staff to enter the leads into your database after the show. Find someone who is familiar with your software, so as to reduce the learning curve (which you pay for), but, more importantly, to speed things up. Check if the organiser can give you the results in an electronic format that will import automatically into your database. This could save you a lot of time.

Using temporary staff may be preferable to using your own, because the latter generally take longer, sometimes exasperatingly so. They are busy with their normal duties, and this is an extra burden that they have to fit in. If you do use your own staff, however, ensure that they have been part of the planning process, that they understand what is happening and the timelines they are working to, and arrange extra time for them to dedicate to this task.

The A list, in particular, has to be processed at once, and the follow-up letters sent out within a day or so of the show.

## Using the database to monitor sales

In some ways the most important reason for maintaining an electronic database is that it makes it much easier to monitor sales from the show and get some meaningful feedback on the results. This in turn allows you to do a return-on-investment calculation on the show after the sales results are in, and so decide if it is worth going into again. More on this in Chapter 14, *Three months after the show*.

## Using the organiser's database

If you can get a database of all the show visitors from the organiser, and if it can be meaningfully searched via fields that are relevant to you, it may be a very rich source of potential clients missed at the show.

It may be easier to search if you can import the entries into your own database software. Check if the organiser can give you the database in a compatible format, or if your software can do the conversion. Otherwise, there are software houses specialising in conversion for a fee.

# Analysing the show

Since you are having this meeting within a day or so of the show, it is the best time to review it, while it's still fresh in everyone's mind. There are a number of areas you may want to address: the stand, the product display, the staffing and the number and quality of the show visitors.

## How did our stand perform?

There are a number of key questions that you can ask about the stand—all of them, of course, with a view to improving it next time.

- How did it look? Did it convey the desired image of our company? Was it inviting for people to come onto? Did it stop people in the aisle? How did it do these things?
- Was it big enough? Was it big enough during busy periods?
- How did it help us? How did it effectively sell our product or service to visitors who were unattended while we were all busy? How did the display help us in persuading potential buyers while we were talking to them?
- How was the position? Was there a good traffic flow past our stand?
- How can we improve things next time?

## How effective was our product display?

Here, too, there are key questions you can ask and, as with the stand, the purpose is to determine how to improve next time.

- What did we have displayed? What should we leave out next time and what should we add?
- How were our products or services presented and displayed? What worked? What didn't? In what ways were the displays attractive? In what ways were they informative? How was the information we wanted them to have delivered to an unattended person?
- What drew visitors and what did not? What drew the most visitors? How? What kind of visitors did it draw? How can we draw more of our target visitors?
- How did the displays empower us so that our presentations were more effective?
- How can we improve next time?

## How effective was our stand staffing?

- How can we improve our performance next time?
- How did we look? If others looked better than us, why?
- How long were people rostered on for? How did this affect performance? Did we take enough breaks so that we stayed reasonably fresh and didn't get too tired?
- Were the right people on the stand?
- How many leads did each person get? Did each person have a target to reach? Does each person know how they performed?
- How confident were we about what we were supposed to do? Did all the people who staffed the stand attend training sessions on our products? Did all the staff attend training sessions on how to handle show visitors? Were we all clear on who was our target market for this show? Did we learn and practise techniques for interviewing and qualifying stand visitors?
- How many sales were made on the stand? How many leads were generated? Were the lead forms properly filled out? Which is more effective, making sales on the stand or generating leads?
- What parts of our presentations were effective? What could we have done to make them more effective? Were we customer-focused or product-focused?

## What were the numbers and quality of show visitors?

The key to a show is the quantity and quality of the show visitors. However, unless you have a product that appeals to everyone, it is not the total number of visitors that is important, but the total number of your target market.

The *quality* is determined by how closely those visitors approach the specific people you want to reach, namely the buyers of your products.

This discussion needs to be put into context. It is easy to talk about what the visitors were like (and often quite fun!), but remember that these reactions are based on personal feelings and experiences. It is also easy to unfairly blame the exhibition and the organiser when the problem may really lie with the inadequate planning carried out by the exhibitor.

Nevertheless, it is a fact that some shows are poor, either overall, or for individual exhibitors, while others have an embarrassment of riches.

But in the final analysis, how good a show was can only be determined after the results of the follow-up process are in. The figures tell the story.

# Chapter 12

# For the two weeks following the show

- **Follow up the A list**
- **Timing of the letters and calls**
- **Do the mail-out to the B list**

# Follow up the A list

The two weeks following the show constitute the period during which your salespeople need to follow up their A list leads.

The procedure is:

1. Send out the follow-up letters
2. Distribute their lists to the salespeople
3. The salespeople phone the contacts from their list

## Send out the follow-up letters

Once you have your leads entered into your database, you can send out the letters. If you get good customer-tracking software, it will perform an automatic mail-merge of the leads, personally addressing them to the recipients.

The leads can also be coded A and B, and appropriate letters sent to each. You can, in addition, code which leads have been given to each salesperson, and individual letters can be printed off for each one. These are then signed by the salespeople and sent off with brochures or other material.

You will have already written the follow-up letters, as outlined in Chapter 5, one each for the A and the B lists, and they are waiting in your word processor.

The A list letters basically say three things: thank you for visiting our stand, I have enclosed a brochure, and I will be in touch very soon. The B list letters—if you want to send them—will not have the part about being in touch very soon, but will include an invitation to contact you if you can be of further help.

The follow-up letter is very important because:

1. It makes you look professional and efficient. You have been paying attention and you have followed up. This speaks for the likely level of your service and reliability.
2. Given the effectiveness of the follow-up procedures of most companies, you will probably be the only one the prospective client spoke to at the show who actually gets in touch. You have a jump on your competition.
3. It introduces the salesperson (or reintroduces him or her if they already made contact on the stand).

4. It is another contact. If the recipient is one of those who was invited to the stand prior to the show, then this is the fourth contact. And if it takes five contacts, on average, to get a new client, then the next meeting will likely result in a sale.

5. It gives the salesperson a reason to ring ('Just ringing to make sure you got the letter'), and provides a natural opening into the rest of the conversation. The purpose of the call is, of course, to make a sale or, as is more often the case, an appointment.

## Distribute their individual lists to the salespeople

When you have keyed the A list sales leads into the database (which should happen within a day), and coded them with the individual salespeople's names, it should be a simple matter to print each person's individual follow-up list.

These lists will probably be different to the ones your salespeople have been used to. They may have memories of being given badly qualified leads that generate very disappointing results, such as piles of business cards that came out of competitions with broadly appealing prizes (as opposed to prizes that are of interest only to your target market). Typically, in such situations, they quickly become discouraged with the poor response they are getting and turn back to their normal activity.

This time, however, your salespeople will be given a comparatively short list of qualified leads sorted into priority order, and they will find they have a high success rate. They will feel that they are on a winning streak and become more confident, and this in turn will generate more sales, for self-confidence has been shown to be the single element most predictive of success in many areas.

It may be worthwhile, therefore, to remind them that this list contains well-qualified prospects, and that a high proportion of them will become customers if approached.

Incidentally, you are likely to find that performance picks up at the next show. Not only will your salespeople be better at managing visitors, but they will be more enthusiastic, having seen the positive results of their previous efforts.

## Establish criteria for performance

When you distribute the leads to your staff, you also have the list yourself in your database, which allows you to monitor progress and results. Importantly, it also allows you to monitor individual salespeople's activity. They need to understand that they only have a two-week window of opportunity to follow up these leads. While there is a *two-month* window in which they will make the bulk of their sales, the *setting up* of those sales needs to happen in the few *weeks* after the show.

The follow-up letters will reach their contacts within two or three days after the end of the show and your people need to begin ringing a couple of days after that. In other words, they should start ringing the people on their lists five days after the show finishes.

Schedule meetings with them at which they will report back on the results. I would recommend that the first two meetings happen weekly, and subsequent ones fortnightly.

Depending on the product, there is a pattern to after-show sales. Unless the product or service has a long lead time, most sales arising from a show are made within the two months following it. The number of completed sales follows a normal distribution curve, with the bulk happening between the third and sixth weeks.

Note that we are not saying this is when these new clients are *contacted*. Rather, this is when the sales are *completed*. . . . That is why it's important for the salespeople to get back to the potential buyers very soon after the show, so that they can start making appointments.

## The salespeople phone the contacts on their list

Having their lists, the salespeople can now ring the people on them. Their approach is very natural: 'Just ringing to see if you've got the letter I sent you.'

The calls should be fairly straightforward. You already know that these people have expressed an interest in your product. You are simply following up on that expressed interest and suggesting the next step. Depending on your product, this may be to make an appointment to see the person again, or in fact to make a sale over the phone.

If the person has received the letter but not yet looked at it, the salesperson asks if they would like a few more days to look at it, or would like to meet anyway. If they have not received it, the salesperson offers to re-send it, or better still, to fax it immediately, perhaps along with the brochure, and to ring back the following day. Or perhaps the person is willing to make the appointment anyway. It does not hurt to ask.

## Timing of the letters and calls

Some companies send leads from the show back to the office each day to have them entered into the database, so that follow-up letters can be sent out straight away. Others wait until after the show, as has been described above.

For most companies, doing it after the show works well. Unless you are collecting a very large number of leads each day (in which case you may want to process them as you go), doing it after the show will get your follow-up letter to the stand visitor within about three days of the show, with a follow-up phone call about five days after the show.

You need not be too concerned about your competitors getting there before you, as experience suggests that few companies have any kind of systematic follow-up procedure. So you will probably be the only one to get in touch after the show, anyway. However, it is best not to be complacent because some industries seem to be more on the ball than others.

If any potential client needs a quicker contact than this, you will probably have picked that fact up at the show and either tagged the lead or separated it out and ensured that the person was contacted immediately.

## Do the mail-out to the B list

The approaches to following up the people on the B list were covered in the previous chapter.

# Chapter 13

# For two months after the show

- Following up and selling
- The pattern of after-show sales
- The pattern of contacts
- Rates of success
- What happens after the two-month period?

# Following up and selling

During the two months following the show, there should be a concentration on following up the leads, as outlined in the previous two chapters, and making sales.

## The pattern of after-show sales

As was mentioned earlier, there is a pattern to after-show sales. Most are made within a couple of months after it. The number of completed sales follows a normal distribution curve, with the bulk of them happening between the third and the sixth week.

This is not the case with some products, of course, as they have longer lead times. One of my clients supplies and maintains the climate control systems in large buildings. These are installed during the building process, and need to be specified well ahead of time, during the design of the building. The lead times for getting new clients for this suite of products and services can be years.

However, even with these kinds of show visitors, the salespeople still need to get back to them immediately after the show, so as to start the long-term process of winning them over.

For those products which have a shorter sales cycle, it is even more important for the prospective clients to be contacted immediately after the show. While the sale itself may be made a month or so after the show, there need to be contacts and sales calls in the meantime to set those sales up. This should happen in the week or two after the show. If the salespeople are quick enough, they may be able to complete the sale before competitors even get around to the initial contact.

## The pattern of contacts

There is a common understanding that it takes five contacts, on average, to get a new client. And indeed, often the only difference between a good salesperson and an ordinary one is that the good one keeps going back after the ordinary one gives up. As they say, 80% of success is showing up.

Now consider the contact process that we have been following. A potential client on your original personal invitation lists got a phone call inviting them to meet you, then a letter confirming the meeting, then the meeting on the stand, then the letter after the show, then the phone call to follow up the letter and make the appointment. When you sit down with the person again, it is the sixth contact and the second face-to-face meeting!

Even for the person you met on the stand for the first time, this is the fourth contact.

And your opposition? Well, if the follow-up procedure of most companies is a guide, they aren't even in contact with the person. But don't relax. They might be.

## Rates of success

Are you going to win every job? No. Are you increasing your chances? Definitely. The tactics described in this book are aimed at making an improvement at every step in the process of winning new clients at exhibitions, and progressive improvements have a cumulative effect.

Companies have literally transformed their exhibition activity from operations of dubious benefit to powerful profit centres that everyone looks forward to.

## What happens after the two-month period?

The purpose of this two-month period of activity is to concentrate your effort on hot sales leads, the A list. Any lead that takes longer than this to close falls into regular sales activity, and is treated as any normal lead.

At the end of this two-month period of active selling, you will know what business has come in from the show and perhaps have a pretty good idea of what is still to come. Now you can do a cost/benefit or return-on-investment analysis of the show. That is covered in the next chapter.

## Signage
### Free ET Tips
Convention Special

Demonstration          teachers only monitor
  Benefits ↑ productivity in lessons
         $ best for their students
      (not all teachers - only the best).
         offer most
  Why do ear training? -

Customer interview to determine
  buyers - potential etc
       Pg 95-96
    1 kind of exam or evaluation
              system to you use
           ? RACE + AP. - University
    2 ET n SS in program
    3 level of students in studio

Booth dialogue - 104

Equipment - more lights?
         stapler
         follow up lead forms Pg 100
             sales forms

# Chapter 14

# Three months after the show

- The difficulty of measuring the benefits of exhibiting
- Do a return-on-investment analysis of the show
- Review your targets and set new ones
- Circulate a report on the results
- Celebrate and reward success!

# The difficulty of measuring the benefits of exhibiting

One of the great difficulties clients report is with assessing the benefits of exhibiting. They cannot quantify the results. While the costs are easy enough, it is often difficult to determine the amount of business the show has actually generated.

If you have come to this point in implementing the system of exhibiting described in this book, you should now have sufficient data to make a hard assessment of the benefits of the show. However, this may depend on the nature of your sales cycle. If it is such that the selling of your products and services has a long lead time, you may have to wait longer than three months before you can do an analysis. For some products and services, as we have said, the lead time can be years.

But if yours is a more conventional business, you can now:

1. Do a return-on-investment analysis of the show
2. Determine if you have reached your targets
3. Establish a target for next year's show, and prepare a preliminary budget
4. Circulate a report of the results.

# Do a return-on-investment analysis of the show

By now all your costs should be in hand, and if your business follows the normal two-month selling cycle and you have a system in place for monitoring your sales results, you will have a good idea of the business you got from the show.

For business that is still in the pipeline, ask your salespeople to give you a percentage likelihood of getting it. Or you may know what percentage of leads/presentations end up in business, and you can use that as a guide.

What about those new customers that saw your products at the show and contacted you independently? Easy. Just ensure that your sales people ask *every* new customer how they heard of you.

## Lifetime value of your clients

It is important when calculating the sales figures from the show that you take into account the lifetime value of any new clients you have gained. The lifetime value of a client is the average value of his purchases over the whole lifetime of your business relationship. So, as an example, if an average individual sale is $500, and these are usually made about five times a year, and your clients stay with you for an average of six years before they move away, then the lifetime value of your clients is $15,000. It can be quite an eye-opening experience for companies who do this calculation for the first time, incidentally. It suddenly makes them value their clients a little more highly.

It is more realistic to measure returns from a show using lifetime value, rather than just taking immediate sales into account. From this perspective, shows are often more profitable than was first thought.

Since you now have both costs and sales available for the show, you can calculate the returns on your marketing investment. And now you can, at last, make a rational decision about whether to keep exhibiting in this particular show.

## Review your targets and set new ones

With the results of the show in hand, you can establish a target for next year's show, and prepare a preliminary budget. Look back over the aims and targets you set for the show in the initial planning stages. Did you reach them, exceed them or fall short? With the information you now have, you can set more realistic goals for future shows.

And given that your team members, with their new skills, are now probably performing much better than they were previously, your new realistic targets may be much higher than before.

## Circulate a report of the results

It is useful to circulate a short report on the results of the show, just a single page summary, to everyone involved. People like to be kept in the communication loop, and they will also do better next time if they know what they are doing. Talk about it. Talk about next year's targets.

If the results are positive, they will be encouraging and can inspire people to do better. If they are negative, then they should be food for thought and discussion, and perhaps give rise to a determination to do better next time.

## Celebrate and reward success!

Take the show team out to lunch!

Goals ① Sales
② Info - different US systems + how
teachers approach ET + SS
possible new applications

③ Other booths set up

③ Other booths set ups +
marketing ideas

④ Contacts c̄ publishers +
distribution systems


At Stand
- stools
- water

# Index

two weeks before show
   move-in details, reconfirm, 80
   resources and supplies, check, 80
   stand, check, 80
   training, 80–2
Tourist, 94
Trade magazines, advertising, 48
Training, 32
   competitors' products, comparison, 81–2
   product demonstration, 82–7
   product training, 81–2
Transport, 33
Transportation, 76
Travel arrangements, 32
   confirmation, 63
Twelve months before show
   planning, 12
   reasons for exhibiting, 12–19
   resource analysis, 25–6
   stand position, choice, 24–5
   tactics, 7
   target market, definition, 19–20
Two months after show
   after two-month period, 145
   after-show sales pattern, 144
   contacts, pattern, 144–5
   following up and selling, 144
   success rates, 145
   tactics, 8
Two weeks before show
   resources and supplies, check, 80
   stand, check, 80
   tactics, 8
   training, 80–109
Two weeks following show
   A list follow-up, 138–40
   B list mail-out, 141

letters and calls, timing, 141
tactics, 8

**U**
Undemonstrable product/service, 83–4
Uniforms, 53–4

**V**
Venue
   stand design factor, 44
Venue costs, 33
Visibility, 15
Visibility of stand, 39–40
Visiting show
   choosing and assessing show, 22
Visitor categories, identification, 91–4
Visitor incentives, 47
Visitor management skills, 65, 87–8
   before show
     potential clients, invitation, 91
   during show
     visitor categories, identification, 91–4
Visitor tracking system, 103
Visitors *See also* Clients
   details, recording, 99–102
   tracking systems, 103
   unattended, 108

**W**
Watchers
   product demonstrations, 84
Water intake, 110
Water intake of staff during show, 122
Website
   exhibition website, 73
   staff training assistance information, 109